William Lee Trenholm

The People's Money

William Lee Trenholm
The People's Money
ISBN/EAN: 9783744759878
Printed in Europe, USA, Canada, Australia, Japan
Cover: Foto ©ninafisch / pixelio.de

More available books at **www.hansebooks.com**

THE PEOPLE'S MONEY

THE PEOPLE'S MONEY

BY

W. L. TRENHOLM

"Je n'ai point tiré mes principes de mes préjugés, mais de la nature des choses."
"Bien des vérités ne se feront sentir qu' après qu' on aura vu la chaine qui les lie à d'autres."—MONTESQUIEU

NEW YORK
CHARLES SCRIBNER'S SONS
1893

TROW DIRECTORY
PRINTING AND BOOKBINDING COMPANY
NEW YORK

INTRODUCTION

The following pages are written not for the learned, or for those who are versed in economic literature, but for the large number of plain people who desire to get some practical ideas upon the important subject to which they relate.

During the last few years public attention has been very much more occupied with questions of financial legislation than at any other period within the memory of those now living. The magazines and newspapers have been full of information, inquiries, and suggestions in regard to the money system of this country, and these have awakened interest and excited study. No doubt there are to-day many thousands of persons who have become much better informed upon this subject than they were a few years ago, and a still greater number of thousands who desire to be informed upon the subject; and yet there still remain vast multitudes, really intelligent and generally well informed, who cheerfully and rather exultantly profess ignorance of financial matters, and an inability to comprehend the principles which ought to control in financial legislation and the natural laws which govern the operations of trade and exchange. It is for these, especially, that this publication is made.

Many men of moderate means, wholly dependent upon slender investments, and therefore more vitally interested than the rich in the results of financial legislation and administration, go through life contented with their fancied inability to understand the operation of economic laws. This is all the more amazing because such persons must perceive that a knowledge of these matters is possessed by many of their acquaintances to whom they are unwilling to acknowledge intellectual inferiority, and they must know that such knowledge cost these others neither inordinate effort nor prolonged study.

It is the purpose of this treatise to point out the importance of understanding about money, banks, the Treasury, etc., and to enable any person of ordinary education and intelligence to acquire such knowledge of them by attention to familiar experiences and to the contents of the daily newspapers. An understanding of the whole subject of finance may be acquired, with but little time and effort, if only its principles and practical methods are observed, one by one, and in due order of succession.

He who looks at these matters only in a general sort of way, and hastily, will necessarily get his perceptions into a tangle, and will be confused instead of enlightened. Whoever looks in the same way and for the first time at the machinery of a factory in operation, might well suppose himself incapable of understanding definitely and practically the processes by which wool and cotton are made into cloth, amid such a wilderness of wheels. The longer he tries to penetrate, at a single glance, all the movements rapidly passing before his eyes, the more hopeless is he of arriving at a distinct conception of how it is all done. But let him begin at the furnace and follow the successive steps by which the energy of heat is converted into the power that drives the mass of machinery; then let him go to the room where the raw material is unpacked; next to the cards where the fibre is straightened and smoothed; then to the drawing frames where the filaments are run together; and so on past the spindles to the looms, and in an hour or two, what before seemed confusion, will be recognized as the perfection of order; what he thought incomprehensible will be found as simple as threading familiar streets.

To the uneducated it is easier to master the construction and movements of machinery than to learn to read or write; yet the number of persons who can read and write is greater than the number who understand machinery, showing conclusively that in both cases ordinary effort and attention will be rewarded with knowledge. Now, if one looks at the business of sixty million of people in the same way that an uneducated man gapes at a library, or as a novice in machinery gazes for the first time at a great factory in operation, of course the subject will seem incomprehensible.

But since no person of ordinary intelligence is really incapable of learning to read, or unable to understand machinery, surely no such person need doubt his ability to obtain a clear and definite understanding of the financial system of the United States, however complicated it may seem at first sight. In order to reach such an understanding it is necessary to begin at the right point and then to proceed methodically. In learning to read we begin with the alphabet and work up to the book. In learning about manufacturing we begin with the raw material and the elementary processes of its treatment, and follow it through the intermediate stages until it is turned out a finished product. And so in finance, we must begin with the elements of the system, with coins and bank-notes, that pass from hand to hand as cash; with promissory notes and bills of exchange, which are the simplest instruments of credit.

These two, cash and credit, are the component elements of all financial operations; they are like the fibres of silk and wool in tapestry; they are the warp and woof, the web and the filling, the interwoven threads of that fabric, which we call finance. Banks, clearing-houses, even the United States Treasury, in some of its functions, may be regarded as so many machines, used to expedite and to cheapen the weaving together of these threads. The threads themselves—the cash and credits—are brought to the machines by the operations of trade, while the financial fabric into which they are ultimately woven sustains and binds together our extended commerce, domestic and foreign, and these in turn nourish our varied industries, and bring to every door the daily bread on which we live.

The people of the United States, through their representatives in Congress, have full power to control financial legislation; but if this power is not exercised aright there is no way in which mistakes or wilful wrong in monetary or currency legislation can be subsequently corrected without pecuniary loss to the people themselves. In this respect the people of our country are no better off than the Austrians or the Russians. The popular power over a currency already established is, everywhere alike, limited to an expression of distrust in the kind of money provided by the Government, and the expression of this distrust becomes evident and therefore effective only when it produces depreciation of the particular currency distrusted. Of such money there have been frequent examples in the United States.

Before the Revolution, the Colonies issued currency in various forms, which became depreciated because the people lost confidence in its value. The Continental money issued by the United Colonies during the Revolution passed through a process of continuous depreciation, until it became absolutely worthless. During the first half of the present century nearly every State granted charters which empowered banks to issue circulating notes which varied widely in value at different times and places, and many of these notes ultimately became valueless. In no case did the people at large escape the suffering which attends a fluctuating and depreciating currency, even though the final loss fell wholly on the note-holders. Neither the force of law during the colonial period, nor the ardor of patriotism excited by the Revolution, nor that feeling of State pride which was so intense thirty or forty years ago, sufficed to maintain the value of any currency which became tainted with popular distrust.*

During the Revolution the patriotic leaders in that struggle exhausted the art of rhetoric in appeals to their countrymen to sustain the continental currency; the press of the struggling Republic united to excite and to keep alive a popular temper well calculated to terrify and to coerce the recusant citizens who demanded for their labor or their products, a higher price in continental money than they were willing to take in British coins; but neither passionate oratory nor popular feeling could arrest the depreciation of the bills of credit put out by the continental congress, or stay the march of ruin from one end to the other of the politically free and independent United States.

These facts in our own history are striking examples of what has occurred over and over again, in one form or another, both here and in other parts

* In South Carolina, in 1722, twenty-eight of the most prominent and wealthy merchants of Charleston were cited before the bar of the colonial Assembly, upon a charge of contempt. The charge was founded upon a respectful memorial which they had presented to that body protesting against the failure of the Government to carry out its promise to provide for the redemption of the currency. The memorialists were adjudged guilty of contempt, and were actually imprisoned until they individually retracted their statement that the public faith had been violated, and as a further punishment to the whole class represented by these memorialists, the Assembly immediately ordered an additional issue of the very currency against which the memorial was directed. Even these arbitrary proceedings failed to sustain the value of the money in question. They indeed produced the opposite effect; the currency became more depreciated than ever, and in a few months the community was reduced to destitution.

of the world; and all such instances, taken together, establish the principle that public confidence can alone sustain any form of money in undepreciated circulation, and that public confidence can be neither commanded by authority, coerced by violence, nor excited by sentiment. When the choice lay between American paper currency and "British coins," even the fathers of the Republic found themselves compelled to obey the natural law rather than that which they had themselves enacted. The origin of a currency is soon forgotten; its probable future is never lost sight of. Every man's intelligence naturally and necessarily impels him to use every effort to prevent his property and interests from suffering by the use of a currency perceived to be tending toward depreciation; and all men acting upon this common and overmastering impulse produce a force against which decrees and proclamations avail nothing, a force which statutes and courts cannot cope with, and which even cannon and bayonets fail to subdue.

The instances referred to also establish the principle, that a depreciated currency is a positive evil, affecting all classes, reaching every individual, undermining accumulated wealth, producing unhealthy and ruinous speculation, obstructing enterprise, repressing industry, oppressing and defrauding labor, corrupting and impoverishing the entire community. Since we see that the people of the United States have no greater power than the subjects of the Czar to protect themselves against the evils of a depreciated currency, it follows that adequate security against these evils must be taken beforehand, and that it can be obtained only by bringing the force of public opinion to bear upon the legislation of Congress in such a way as to prevent the creation or emission of any currency that can possibly become depreciated. Hence it follows further that public opinion, in order to be effective to this end, must necessarily be founded upon a general knowledge throughout the community of the principles which should underlie and control such legislation, and upon a practical acquaintance with the manner in which these principles are to be maintained.

TABLE OF CONTENTS

PAGE

INTRODUCTION, ... v

CHAPTER I.
INDUSTRY, COMMERCE, FINANCE, AND THE PEOPLE, . 1

CHAPTER II.
CASH AND CREDIT, ... 13

CHAPTER III.
MONEY, . . 22

CHAPTER IV.
NATURAL BASIS OF MONEY, 37

CHAPTER V.
INDUSTRIAL BASIS OF MONEY, . . 45

CHAPTER VI.
LAW AS A BASIS OF MONEY, . . 51

CHAPTER VII.
CONFIDENCE AS A BASIS OF MONEY, . 60

CHAPTER VIII.

DEFINITENESS AND STABILITY OF VALUE, THE SOLE ESSENTIAL QUALITIES OF MONEY, . . . 78

CHAPTER IX.

THE MONETARY UNIT, ... 90

CHAPTER X.

LEGAL TENDER, ... 109

CHAPTER XI.

THE MATERIAL AND FORM OF MONEY, . 116

CHAPTER XII.

COINED MONEY, ... 130

CHAPTER XIII.

PAPER MONEY, ... 141

CHAPTER XIV.

TREASURY-NOTE, OR DUE-BILL CIRCULATION, . . 152

CHAPTER XV.

BANK-NOTE CIRCULATION, . . . 162

CHAPTER XVI.

THE BALANCE OF TRADE, ... 190

CHAPTER XVII.

PAGE

The Volume of Money, ... 199

CHAPTER XVIII.

Value, ... 225

CHAPTER XIX.

The Standard of Value, . . . 238

CHAPTER XX.

The Gold Standard, . . 258

Conclusion, ... 275

In order to put industry into motion, three things are requisite: materials to work upon, tools to work with, and the wages or recompense, for the sake of which the work is done.

Money is neither a material to work upon, nor a tool to work with; and although the wages of the workman are commonly paid to him in money, his real revenue, like that of all other men, consists not in the money, but in the money's worth; not in the metal pieces, but in what can be got for them.—ADAM SMITH, p. 120.

THE PEOPLE'S MONEY

CHAPTER I.

INDUSTRY, COMMERCE, FINANCE, AND THE PEOPLE

This is essentially an industrial age, and in no country of the world is industry more universal or more varied than it is in the United States. Here nearly everybody is either an industrial worker, with brain or sinew, or is maintained by some such worker. A vast majority of the population work for wages, salaries, fees, or commissions, or else they produce something for sale. In every case the object sought by these workers is what is familiarly termed "making a living," or "making money." Few persons can afford to give time, labor, or talents for nothing; all, or very nearly all, are intent upon earnings or profits, and generally these can be acquired only in the form of money. To acquire money, therefore, is in a measure forced upon every worker, because few are so situated as to be able to produce the articles essential to their sustenance and comfort, while none can produce all they habitually use and consume in the way of clothing, shelter, food, fuel, and medicine, not to speak of such quasi-necessaries as newspapers, books, and recreation.

So many million industrial workers could not be employed profitably and constantly, were it not for what Adam Smith termed "the division of labor," but what may be termed, more accurately, perhaps, in our day, "the specialization of employments." It is because the employments of modern industry have become varied and specialized that each worker is able to find continuous occupation in producing something or doing something beyond what is adapted to his own use or needs. The excess, indeed generally the whole, of what is thus done or produced, by the multitude of individuals, becomes more or less widely distributed throughout the community, and in some cases over the whole world, through the agency of trade and commerce.

The distribution effected by these agencies results in a general interchange of services and industrial products, and such an interchange is essential to the maintenance of the very specialization of employments from which it arises, because individual workers devoting themselves exclusively, each to what he can do best, have no other reliance but this interchange for severally obtaining what they want, but do not make, in exchange for what they make, but do not use. It is evident, therefore, that communities industrially organized as ours is, on the principle of the specialization of employments, consist almost wholly of individuals who are dependent from day to day upon trade and commerce to carry on that ceaseless interchange by which alone each converts what he has, but does not want, into what he wants, but lacks. Trade and commerce effect the interchange of industrial products and services by the use of money, or its substitute, credit, employing these as counters or "chips," which being paid or pawned for services or commodities contributed to the common stock, are redeemable in other services or commodities drawn out of the common stock.

From the commercial point of view money is a receipt for value and an order for value, both in one, just as an elevator certificate, which primarily is a receipt for a definite quantity or weight of grain, serves also as an order upon the elevator company for a like quantity or weight of grain of the same kind and grade. Commerce deals wholly in services and commodities, rating these according to their respective values, and it employs money or credit simply as the medium or vehicle by means of which these values are exchanged one for another. Finance, on the other hand, deals in money and credit as values in themselves distinct from their function of representing, and so conveying value in other things. To use a homely illustration, commerce may be likened to a storage and transfer company, with the world for its territory, while finance supplies the teams, wagons, trains, and ships by which the transfer operations are carried on.

The transfer managers are intent only upon selecting the best route and the safest and most expeditious carrier, while each carrier looks after his horses and vans, his locomotives and cars, his steamers and ships, without giving any thought as to the owners, the destination, or the contents of the boxes and bales that make up the load or cargo. Thus the merchant buys, sells, and ships his goods in each case, paying or receiving payment in cash, credit, or bills of exchange, according to their respective degrees of availability, and the bankers furnish these as they may be needed by the merchants, without taking note of the commercial operations effected by them. Now, between the transfer agent and the carrier all transactions resolve themselves into terms of weight or bulk, or both, because weight and bulk are the only things about a car-load or a cargo in which there can always be a relation established between shipper and carrier; so between commerce and finance the only common term, into which all their relations may be resolved is value, because value is the only quality common to all the objects dealt in by commerce and finance respectively; that is to say, on the one hand, services and commodities, on the other, money and credits.

Prices form the connecting link between commerce and finance; for the price of a service or of a thing is the expression of its money equivalent at the time and place of its passing from one person to another, and the aggregate of commodities handled and of services rendered within a given area and during a definite period of time, multiplied by the prices paid therefor, measures both the commercial and the financial activity prevailing within those limits.

Two forces are in ceaseless operation, compelling activity in both the commercial and financial worlds, and these forces are demand and supply. Commercial demand springs from the wants of mankind; commercial supply flows from the universality of productive industry. Financial demand arises out of the need of capital in productive industry and in the operations by which trade and commerce are incessantly administering supplies to demands; and financial supply is furnished by accumulated capital in the form of money or credit. The relation between the supply of, and demand for, services and commodities, respectively, determines their several commercial values; the relation between the supply of money and the demand for it (modified by the extent to which credit can be substituted for money) determines financial values, and within limits, which will hereafter be explained, the relation between commercial values and financial values determines prices.

Thus finance and commerce together adjust prices to services and commodities upon a basis of comparative values; and, by means of prices, each man knows how much his own talents and energies will enable him to command in the products of the energies and talents of others. Prices are invariably expressed in money, and hence money, besides being the medium of exchange, is also the general measure of values. Money thus measures the value of everything upon which a price can be put, and this includes not only property and produce and commodities of all kinds, but professional skill and services, literary and other intellectual efforts, and all labor performed for wages, salary, or other money consideration. Every industrial worker earning anything at all must submit to having his work or his services measured by the money in which he is paid, or which is the basis of his payment.

It is because of its function as a measure of value, or more obviously a gauge of prices, that the money we use becomes of immense consequence to us. The little cash we ordinarily have about our persons may be in any form that passes current, because that suffices to make it a medium of exchange; but whether we handle any money at all or not, whether we ever see money or not, makes not the least difference in our absolute dependence upon whatever money is in use as the measure of values or gauge of prices at the time and place at which we live and work. Indeed, the less property a man owns, and the more dependent he is upon his daily efforts for a livelihood, the more vital is his interest in the instrument by which those efforts are measured. If all the money in general circulation is good money, every man is assured of full value for his labor and property; but bad money is never an equivalent for what it takes to get it, and the poor man is never able to choose the money in which he will be paid. The bankers and capitalists may stipulate for gold, or any other medium of payment, but not so the ordinary workers, for they live by specialized employments, and these compel them to pursue their callings from day to day, and to accept compensation in whatever money may be in circulation, because they depend upon that money for buying food, clothing, etc., and they cannot postpone supplying themselves and their families with these necessaries.

The industrial state in which we live places us all under contract to the world's commerce to deliver all we can produce, and to take in exchange all we consume, both to be measured by money, which, since it must be paid out as soon as it is received, may be regarded as only temporarily confided to us for the purpose of exchanging our products or services for those of others. While this money is a receipt for the value of what we produce or do, and an order for equivalent value in other things, it is also the measure or gauge of these values. In other words, it is the dollar's worth and not the dollar itself that on the one hand we work for, and that on the other hand we enjoy in recompense for our efforts.

Now it must be evident that if a person works under a contract to deliver any kind of commodity by the yard or the pound, and to receive in return other commodities by the yard or pound, he has a right to honest weights and measures, and especially he needs to be assured beforehand that the same measurements and weights which are applied to what he delivers are also applied to what he is to receive; hence, on the same principle, every industrial worker has a right to honest money, and needs to be assured that his work is going to be paid for in dollars of identically the same value as the dollars he is compelled to pay out for what he consumes. So important is it that money should be permanent in value that in all civilized countries the regulation of it is one of the prerogatives of sovereignty, and history shows that there is hardly any prerogative of which the intelligent and provident exercise is so far-reaching in its effects.

Under our Constitution Congress alone possesses the power to "regulate the value of money," and this power is exercised by means of the coinage and currency laws which establish what shall be money. The responsibility thus thrown upon Congress is very great, because, in the first place, as has been said already, nearly everybody is interested, and in the second place the industrial masses cannot protect themselves against the consequences of unwise monetary legislation. All of us must submit to having the value of our labor, produce, etc., measured by whatever dollars Congress authorizes, and very few persons, comparatively, are able to ascertain whether these dollars are really of full value. As long as other people take them from us at full value we are satisfied; but if any particular dollars should at any moment of time be discovered not to be of full value they can thenceforward be passed off only at a depreciation, and consequently whoever at that time happens to have any of them will suffer loss; but what is much worse and much more far-reaching, all who have been paid in such money from the inception of the depreciation will have been suffering loss without perhaps knowing to what to attribute it, and all who have accepted old prices for their labor or goods or property, or agreed to furnish them at such prices, will have suffered also, and this includes all persons on fixed salaries, or who are employed on permanent wages.

History records many instances of a currency becoming depreciated, and in every instance the laboring classes, small traders, professional men, farmers, and the like, have been the chief victims. These persons constitute the bulk of every community, and they seldom have the knowledge, skill, or opportunity to protect themselves from loss from a depreciating currency; while merchants, whose transactions are on a large scale, bankers, and capitalists in large cities, not only possess the knowledge which enables them to detect signs of approaching depreciation, but they have also the skill and opportunity to "hedge" against it, besides having access to facilities for applying their skill and knowledge in such a way as to enrich themselves under the very conditions which are ruinous to all other classes.*

Reason and history alike prove conclusively that

* "It may well be doubted," says Macaulay in his *History of England*, Chapter xxi., " whether all the misery which had been inflicted on the English nation in a quarter of a century by bad Kings, bad Ministers, bad Parliaments, and bad Judges, was equal to the misery caused in a single year by bad crowns and bad shillings. Those events which furnish the best theme for pathetic or indignant eloquence are not always those which most affect the happiness of the great body of the people. The misgovernment of Charles and James, gross as it had been, had not prevented the common business of life from going steadily and prosperously on. While the honor and independence of the state were sold to a foreign power, while chartered rights were invaded, while fundamental laws were violated, hundreds of thousands of quiet, honest, and industrious families labored and traded, ate their meals and lay down to rest in comfort and security. Whether Whigs or Tories, Protestants or Jesuits were uppermost, the grazier drove his beasts to market, the grocer weighed out his currants, the draper measured out his broadcloth, the hum of buyers and sellers was as loud as ever in the towns, the harvest-home was celebrated as joyously as ever in the hamlets, the cream overflowed the pails of Cheshire, the apple-juice foamed in the presses of Herefordshire, the piles of crockery glowed in the furnaces of the Trent, and the barrows of coal rolled fast along the timber railways of the Tyne. But when the great instrument of exchange became thoroughly deranged, all trade, all industry were smitten as with a palsy. The evil was felt daily and hourly in almost every place and by almost every class, in the dairy and on the threshing-floor, by the anvil and the loom, on the billows of the ocean and in the depths of the mine. Nothing could be purchased without a dispute. Over every counter there was wrangling from morning to night. The workman and his employer had a quarrel as regularly as the Saturday came round. On a fair-day or on a market-day the clamors, the reproaches, the taunts, the curses were incessant ; and it was well if no booth was overturned and no head brok-

money liable to depreciation is bad money for the people at large. The longer it circulates at full value the worse and more wide-spread will be the evil. No merchant would contract to deliver goods without making some stipulation about the quality of the coin in which he was to be paid. Even men of business were often bewildered by the confusion into which all pecuniary transactions were thrown. The simple and the careless were pillaged without mercy by extortioners whose demands grew even more rapidly than the money shrank. The price of the necessaries of life, of shoes, of ale, of oatmeal, rose fast. The laborer found that the bit of metal, which, when he received it was called a shilling, would hardly, when he wanted to purchase a pot of beer or a loaf of rye bread, go as far as sixpence. Where artisans of more than usual intelligence were collected in great numbers, as in the dockyard at Chatham, they were able to make their complaints heard and to obtain some redress. But the ignorant and helpless peasant was cruelly ground between one class which would give money only by tale and another which would take it only by weight. Yet his sufferings hardly exceeded those of the unfortunate race of authors. Of the way in which obscure writers were treated we may easily form a judgment from the letters, still extant, of Dryden to his bookseller, Tonson. One day Tonson sends forty brass shillings, to say nothing of clipped money. Another day he pays a debt with pieces so bad that none of them will go. The great poet sends them all back, and demands in their place guineas at twenty-nine shillings each 'I expect,' he says in one letter, 'good silver, not such as I have had formerly.' 'If you have any silver that will go,' he says in another letter, 'my wife will be glad of it. I lost thirty shillings or more by the last payment of fifty pounds.' These complaints and demands which have been preserved from destruction only by the eminence of the writer, are doubtless merely a fair sample of the correspondence which filled all the mail-bags of England during several months.

In the midst of the public distress one class prospered greatly, the bankers; and among the bankers none could in skill or in luck bear a comparison with Charles Duncombe. He had been, evils manifesting themselves as soon as its defects are revealed, and sooner or later a defective currency will surely be detected and become depreciated. The only safeguard to the people against the evils of bad money is intelligent and prudent legislation; but in order to insure this in our country the people themselves must understand financial matters, for without this knowledge they cannot distinguish between such of their representatives as counsel wisely and such as are led off by chimeras, nor is it to be expected that representatives will vote and act on the whole with any greater degree of intelligence than that which prevails in the constituencies from which they come, and to which alone they feel accountable.

not many years before, a goldsmith of very moderate wealth. He had probably, after the fashion of his craft, plied for customers under the arcades of the Royal Exchange, had saluted merchants with profound bows, and had begged to be allowed the honor of keeping their cash. But so dexterously did he now avail himself of the opportunities of profit which the general confusion of prices gave to a money-changer that, at the moment when the trade of the kingdom was depressed to the lowest point, he laid down near ninety thousand pounds for the estate of Helmsley, in the North Riding of Yorkshire."

CHAPTER II.

CASH AND CREDIT

Everybody is familiar with the terms "Cash and Credit," as ordinarily used and understood. In cash transactions delivery and payment are simultaneous, while in credit transactions payment is more or less deferred. Accepting this distinction for the present, let each reader reckon up how much in coins, bills, and notes, *i.e.*, actual money, passes out of or into his hands in connection with his business, his investments, and his household and personal expenditures, then let him compute what amounts are represented by checks, collections or payments by others, offsets in accounts, etc., and he will be surprised to find how small a proportion the former amount bears to the latter.

If anyone, after making these computations, will compare results with two other persons, one whose aggregate receipts and expenditures are greater, and another in whose case the amounts are less than in his, he will find that the more a man receives and pays the smaller is the percentage of actual money handled by him. The immense transactions in stocks, exchange, and merchandise at New York, London, and other great centres, are all settled by checks, and these checks are settled again through clearing-houses, so that very little money passes even in the final adjustment of balances. It is highly probable that if every coin, note, and bank-bill in any given community at some moment of time could be located, much the larger part in amount, outside of what is in bank and in the tills of tradesmen, refreshment places, and railroad offices, would be found in the possession of the poorer families.

Of course there is no way of verifying this conjecture, but it rests on these grounds:

1st. The poorer families generally include a decided majority of the community.

2d. Each member of such families generally receives and spends separately his or her income, while the money comes to such persons in small amounts, at short intervals, and is seldom sufficient in amount to be deposited in bank. On the other hand, the head of a well-to-do family receives or supplies the means for all, keeps it in bank, disburses it by checks, buys for the whole family, chiefly on credit, and gives to each member only the money required for small personal expenditures.

3d. The poorer a man is, the less his credit. Those families whose credit suffices for their supplies for a month, need less money *per capita* than those who must buy from day to day and pay as they buy, the bare needs of subsistence being very nearly alike in all classes.

4th. Real estate agents find as a fact that their poorer tenants pay their rents in money, while the others pay in checks.

From these considerations and others of a like nature, it is apparent that in every community the poorer classes handle more actual money than the richer classes, a fact not generally recognized because we are accustomed to think and speak of money being owned, paid, and received in a great many cases in which no money at all is either possessed or handled.

If your bank account shows a balance in your favor you say you have so much money in bank, while in truth you have no money in bank. All the money (coin, bank-bills, etc.) in a bank belongs to the corporation, constitutes part of its assets, hence no fraction of it can belong to any individual depositor. The moment the teller receives your deposit and enters its amount in your pass-book, that moment the *money* you have handed him ceases to be yours and becomes the money of the bank; the very next moment it may be paid to some one else, who takes it out of the bank altogether, and though this is done under your eyes, you do not dream of objecting, though you surely would interfere if you saw any one carrying off bonds you had deposited in that bank, or if you should know of any one using a horse you have at livery. Hence there is a fundamental difference between money and other things; anything else committed to another's custody remains specifically the property of the depositor, but money deposited in bank is parted with as absolutely as when it is paid for a purchased article; in the one case the purchaser has the article, and in the other the depositor has the entry in his pass-book, but the money itself is gone in the one case as much as in the other.

This entry in the pass-book represents, as due from the bank, a sum of money equal to that deposited, not the same money but its equivalent, and as long as the bank meets its obligations the depositor feels secure of getting that amount whenever he asks for it, but if the bank should fail he cannot get it. Suppose the sum to be $100, and that owing $100 he gives his creditor a check on the bank for that amount. Speaking familiarly, one would say he paid all his money on that debt, whereas he did not pay money at all. The proof of this is that if the bank fails before the check can be presented there, he will still have to pay that debt, whereas, if he had paid it in money it would have been extinguished. What a man has in bank, therefore, is not money, but it may be called "money-at-credit."

As in ordinary cases the distinction between money proper and money at credit is not observed, so the term "cash" has become considerably warped from its specific use as the antithesis of credit, for many so-called "cash transactions" are settled monthly, and in some trades the term even covers settlement by note bearing interest.

Although money at credit is now generally called "cash," still, strictly speaking, the term "cash" is applicable only to money, and all transactions rest on credit, except those balanced by a payment in cash at the moment the transaction is made. It is important to observe this distinction, for most readers will be astonished to find how immense is the preponderance, both in numbers and amount, of credit over cash transactions in every community, and how greatly the use of credit economizes the use of money.

It will also surprise many to discover that as a general thing those who give credit are more numerous than those who receive it, and that the aggregate wealth of all the creditors in a community is generally less than that of all the debtors. Here, again, it is impossible to demonstrate the proposition, but it rests on grounds that cannot be questioned. Here are some examples:

Every tradesman who charges goods to his customers is their creditor for the amount charged, and they are his debtors. Every person working for wages or salary, who is not paid in advance, gives his employer credit from hour to hour, from day to day, or for weeks or months, as the case may be. Such persons are creditors, and their employer is debtor for the amount of compensation earned up to the moment of payment.

Every depositor in a bank, savings or otherwise, is a creditor of that institution, and every banknote is evidence of debt due by the bank to the holder of the note. So also every greenback or coin note is evidence of so much debt due to the holder by the Government of the United States.

Every person who pays rent in advance becomes a creditor of his landlord; every person who buys a ticket on a railway or steamboat, or who pays his fare on entering a street-car, is a creditor of the transportation company; every buyer of a ticket to a theatre, circus, or other entertainment, is a creditor of the proprietor; every person who prepays postage, express charge, or premiums of insurance, is a creditor.

That these are credit transactions will be evident, as soon as it is considered that in each one of these cases the person who advances his services, money, or goods may fail to receive the salary, wages, service, payment, benefit, or gratification expected and tacitly contracted for, which could not happen in a cash transaction, where payment and performance are simultaneous. Now, since these persons and all others to whom anything is owing, including the comparatively small number who make a business of lending money,* are creditors, obviously in most communities the creditors outnumber the debtors, while it is probable that the aggregate wealth of all the debtors is greater than that of all the creditors, first, be-

---

* Every loan of money upon collateral security is an instance of mutual trust, the borrower trusts the lender with his property in return for being entrusted with the lender's money, and generally the value of the collateral exceeds the amount of the loan.

cause the debtors in the above instances are possessors of wealth, while the creditors are not, and secondly, because wealth is the basis of credit, and the richer the man the more he is able to borrow.

It is evident, therefore, that considerable confusion of ideas has arisen from the inaccurate use of the words "money" and "credit," and that there is a wide-spread popular error as to which are the creditor and which are the debtor classes of the community, an error hurtful to the masses, chiefly because it deceives them as to the extent of their interest in the monetary system of the country and their stake in its moneyed institutions.

A correct understanding of facts leads to these conclusions:

1st. Since money and money-at-credit are habitually regarded as identical, and are used indiscriminately in cash settlements, the theory of a *per capita* supply of currency lacks the foundation usually assumed to underlie it.

2d. Credit represents money-value, not actual cash in hand nor money-at-credit; it is trusting to a future payment of money, and thus it supplements the use of money, and enormously extends the sphere of trade and commerce, besides facilitating a countless number of transactions entering into the conveniences of life.

3d. Credit economizes the use of money by affording time for the same coins, notes, etc., to go about from hand to hand, from bank to bank, and even from city to city, settling successively an immense number of accounts; it also obviates the use of money altogether in the numberless cases in which credits are offset and balanced, one against the other, as happens every day among customers of the same bank and among banks in the same city.

4th. Credit accomplishes all this through the instrumentality of bookkeeping, checks, drafts, bills of exchange, banks of deposit, clearing-houses, and other similar appliances. Without these all business would be cramped, for there is not gold and silver enough in the world to supply the actual money needed for settling the transactions of a single day in New York and London alone, even if all the rest of the world should go without; nor would any system of paper currency possess the flexibility of volume or the stability of value exhibited by the credit systems of Europe and the United States.

5th. These appliances (the banks, etc.) bring the use of credit within reach not only of large commercial and financial operators, but of most people in easy circumstances throughout the United States, thus leaving the bulk of the actual money in the country for the exclusive use of those who are too poor or too little known to obtain or to utilize credit.

6th. These latter classes, though excluded themselves from credit, are, nevertheless, vitally interested in the maintenance and the extension of the credit system, for, whenever credits are curtailed those who habitually use money find themselves in competition with the other classes for the control of what actual money is in circulation, and people who have least credit are always least able to secure what cash they need in case of a "squeeze" in the money market.

This is not the place to prove these propositions; they will all be fully established in the course of the present treatise, but they are introduced here to arrest attention, and to set readers thinking for themselves, which is the only sure antidote to errors and delusions that are traditional, and that are held with the tenacity with which men cling to superstitions and prejudices. The farmers are, in one sense, the great creditor class, for each of them is constantly investing his own capital, and all he can borrow from others, in crops and in live stock. The crop and the stock are debtors to the farmer not only for the capital thus invested, but also for the value of all labor bestowed upon them by the farmer and his family. The farmers, therefore, are vitally interested in our money laws, for there is a long time between sowing and reaping, and the farmer needs to collect from the produce of his fields and flocks and herds as good money as he puts into these investments.

CHAPTER III.

MONEY

Money, in the concrete form of coins, bills, or notes, is the most familiar of objects; but money becomes a mystery as soon as it is thought of, in the abstract, as one of the elements of modern industrial development. Men, women, and children handle money daily, talk about it, think of it, spend it; the great majority are earners of money, borrowers, lenders, sellers, or buyers, yet comparatively few persons, even among bankers and statesmen, can answer satisfactorily to themselves these simple questions: What is money? What is its function or office? What is the source of its power to command persons and things? On what principles should its substance be determined? How is its quantity regulated? How are prices established? Why do prices vary at different times and in different places?

The question, What is money? may seem as puzzling as Pilate's famous question, "What is truth?" but the puzzle in both cases is about words, not things. Invert the questions and apply them to some actual case. Is a certain thing true? Is a certain thing money? Straightway the puzzle vanishes and we know how to seek out answers. Truth is established by evidence; money is recognized by its ability to perform certain functions. Doctrinaires dispute about the meaning of the word "money" because each holds some theory about finance or political economy to which his own particular definition of money is the key; but surely there ought not to be any uncertainty about the meaning of a word in such constant and such universal use; nor is there any uncertainty, except among advocates of opposing theories. Everybody, including these very theorists, recognize money at sight; even children can generally recognize it, or if any one is in doubt about a particular coin or note there is a conclusive test always at hand—will it pass? Will it buy things, or hire persons or property, or pay debts? If it will do all these things exactly as they are done by what is undoubtedly money, then the coin or note in question *is* money.

This is the final test, because from this there is no appeal. (Anything that will pass current,* from hand to hand, throughout a community, buying, hiring, paying debts, is, to all intents and purposes, money.) The community may not be wise in accepting certain things as money and becoming dependent upon them, but that is a very different

---

* This word "current," from the Latin verb "currere," to run, expresses the idea that is in our minds when we say that a coin "passes." Our term currency comes from the same root and includes the same idea.

matter. We are not yet considering what the material and form of money ought to be, that will come later, we have now to determine only to what class of objects the term "money" is familiarly and universally applied, and it is true and safe to say that this term attaches to whatever, as a matter of fact, passes current in buying, hiring, and paying debts. The substantial correctness of this definition is supported by the use of the word in the account of the earliest recorded instance of the intervention of money in the affairs of human life.

In Genesis xxiii. 16, it is told that Abraham paid for a burying-ground in money "current with the merchant." As in Abraham's time money to serve as a valid payment must be "current with the merchant," so also in our time it must be such as will pass among the people, because now everybody buys and sells, hence we are all merchants in one sense, and "current money with the merchant" is equivalent to money that passes among the people.*

Having ascertained how the word money is applied in its common use and acceptation, the obvi-

---

* In the patriarch's time, however, money was seldom used, and there were no coins, hence Abraham's payment had to be made by weighing bars or ingots of silver. It was the fineness of this silver which constituted it "current with the merchant," the genuineness of the shekel weight, too, might have entered into the expression. These two things—fineness and accurate weight—are now secured by means of coinage, which not only greatly facilitates the use of money, but gives to it, as a measure of value, a degree of precision otherwise unobtainable.

ous reflection is that it is the function or office performed that determines the correctness of the appellation in any particular instance, hence we have next to inquire, what is the function or office of money?

Let us deal only with facts of ordinary experience. Take this simple case to begin with: Give a boy a dollar. His first thought is how will he spend it. If he keeps it any time at all it is simply because he wants to consider how he can get the most out of it. He knows that it can command for him a wide range of gratifications, that it may be divided and subdivided, but he also understands that whether spent as a whole or piecemeal, the money must be parted with in order to be enjoyed. When once he has secured a dollar's worth of anything, or of several things combined, the dollar itself will be wholly gone; his top or his knife remains with him, he can use them, enjoy them over and over again, their power to serve or to please is not impaired by its exercise, but every gratification derived from the dollar diminishes the dollar's power to provide further gratifications.

Take another case: Offer a man a dollar to do a certain piece of work for you. His first thought is, can he afford to give you so much of his time, skill, and labor for that amount of money? To decide this question he must put a value upon his time, his labor, and his skill; he must calculate how much of those will be expended upon the job, and then he must measure these combined values by the dollar, because he will not give them to you for less than what he regards as an equivalent. If he decides that the job will consume three half-dollars' worth of his time, skill, and labor, you will have to consider whether, when done, it will be worth to you as much as a dollar and a half of your money, because if you have the work done you must part with your money in payment for it, and you will not give any sum of money for less than its equivalent in your estimation.

Now, when the boy is considering how he will spend his money, and when you and your man are debating with yourselves and each other about the cost of the job, you are all estimating and comparing values, and you are all accepting the dollar, or some definite part of the dollar, as a measure or standard for determining and expressing the values of different things. With the boy it is perhaps a question of spending a "quarter" on the circus rather than for something he can keep or use; with the man it is a question whether he will take your job or a different one for somebody else, or whether he will not indulge himself with a holiday; with you it may be a question between hiring that man or some other man, or else between doing the work yourself and dispensing with it altogether.

In these cases, while the three persons have widely different ends in view, and seem to be influenced by considerations which have little likeness to each other, yet they all three are measuring their needs and desires by money, and are able to express their preferences by subdivisions of a dollar. The habit of measuring by money all that we have and do and desire is so universal that it is unconsciously resorted to the moment an occasion arises for estimating or comparing the degrees of value we attach to different objects of possession or pursuit, and such occasions arise so incessantly that even children and uneducated persons become skilled in determining whether a desired project or thing is, or is not, worth what it costs. To the cases above supposed the intelligent reader will be able, easily, to add others, illustrating other phases of the functions performed by money; but however far the collection and comparison of facts may be carried, all the inferences from them will be found to coincide in establishing the primary functions of money to be these :

1st. To pass from one person to another in exchange for property or in recompense for labor or services.

2d. To measure the value of whatever is obtainable by purchase, hire, or other form of money payment.*

These two functions of money characterize it in every land, and have always characterized it. When Abraham offered to buy Ephron's field he proposed

---

* Money has other functions, some evolved out of these, others imposed upon it by law or custom, all of which will be considered hereafter, but for the present our apprehension of the subject will be facilitated and kept clear by confining attention to what is simple and familiar.

to "pay the full money it is worth," and when he took possession of his purchase he paid in "money current with the merchant." During the eight and thirty centuries intervening between Abraham's epoch and ours, money has come gradually more and more into use, and, *pari passu*, it has become more and more fixed in form and definite in value, but in all that time its functions have been the same, namely, to transfer ownership and to measure values. Nowadays the use of money is well nigh universal, and extends to objects of which the patriarch could form no conception. By money we measure the value of all we sell and all we buy; labor, thought, speech, pleasure, religious opportunities and exercises, sensual gratifications, even vicious indulgences are priced and paid for in money.

Injury to person, property, or reputation, even the tender affections of women, and the precious life of parent, husband, or child, are appraised by juries at a money value. "Insurance against accident and death" means simply a money payment upon the occurrence of either, while the pension laws affix prices upon life, limb, or health lost in the public defence.

As an instrument of purchase and hire, as a measure of value, money, or one of its representatives, enters into every act of industrial production. It enters also into every commercial transaction, for since every purchase is also a sale, and since the same money travels from one to another, effecting numerous such sales by which the products of industry are exchanged among their producers, money serves as the medium of general exchange; and further, since these exchanges rest upon a comparison of respective values, as measured by the money passing in exchange for each commodity, the money also serves as a measure of the value of the commodities.

Whenever money passes in exchange for property, services, etc., its value is presumed to be equal to that of the thing for which it is exchanged, hence the amount of money paid — the price — becomes the expression of the value of that thing. In this respect a dollar is as absolutely a measure of value as an inch is a measure of length, or as a pound is a measure of weight. In many cases, however, values are estimated and expressed in money terms when no money is present, and some persons have found a difficulty in understanding how these can be accepted as instances of the measurement of value by money.

Such difficulty will disappear when it is considered that from the constant use of any standard in actual measurements we acquire more or less skill in estimating similar measurements without applying our standard, and since money is by far the most frequently used of all standards of measurement, it is quite natural that there should be fixed in our minds a value-scale marked off in dollars and fractions of a dollar sufficiently accurate to serve ordinary purposes. In these cases, therefore, while we may not actually measure with money all the values we are dealing in, our estimate and acceptance of these values proceeds wholly from belief in the accuracy of our mental value-scale, and accuracy in this case means, of course, conformity with actual money values.

But apart from this, distance and weights are often computed instead of being ascertained by actually traversing the distance with a rule or rod, and without weighing the object in question. The diameter of the earth at the equator, the distance to the moon from any given point on the earth's surface at some particular moment of time, have been, and can always be, accurately determined. In such cases computation alone is available, since actual measurement with rule or rod is impracticable. The weight of the earth has been ascertained, and that of some of the planets, yet no balance could hold them. In like manner one may accurately estimate values and express them in dollars, even though he may never have had dollars enough to exchange for even a fraction of such values.

The fact is that money performs its function of measuring values chiefly through the medium of computation; it is the standard by reference to which we constantly test and readjust the value-scales which we carry about in our minds, very much as the standards of weight and measurement kept in the National Museum at Washington are referred to for determining or verifying the accuracy of the implements made for ordinary use.

In various parts of the world money is of different substances and forms; but what gives to every form of money all the force it has, what can alone confer upon anything the power to pass unquestioned from hand to hand, exchanging and measuring values, is the confidence and consent of the people among whom it circulates. Imagine this wanting in any given case, and then conjecture, if you can, by what other means or expedient a distrusted or discredited currency could be maintained as a medium of exchange or as a measure of values. It is true that in modern times and among civilized nations governments act for the people in selecting and certifying what is to pass as money, and in fixing by law the values of the different denominations of a monetary system; but except for the settlement of contracts, the payment of debts, and the discharge of public dues, the power of the government to prescribe a currency is absolutely limited by the acquiescence of the people, and stability in the purchasing power of such currency depends from day to day upon the continuance of that acquiescence.

In countries where the laws do not prescribe any particular form of money, the money in use depends for its force entirely upon conventional recognition, and this is always found sufficient. Mere custom, without the help of law, maintained for ages the volume and stability of all the money circulating among the three hundred million people of the Chinese Empire. In very ancient times too, before coinage or paper money was invented, and when money was in very limited use, its force as a measure of value and as a medium of purchase and sale, was necessarily derived from usage alone.

The passage already referred to, about Abraham's purchase, shows that more than three thousand seven hundred years ago, the ownership of property was habitually transferred upon payment of "the full money it is worth," and also, that the medium of such payments was "current money with the merchant."

To facilitate interchange of values and to measure such values may be regarded as the natural functions of money, but in most civilized countries it has another function, which is artificial and established by law, viz., that of a legal tender in payment of taxes and in discharge of debt. Debt is a product of civilization, it can arise only where credit exists and where law prevails, because where those conditions are wanting men do not trust each other and hence there are neither debtors nor creditors, for manifestly no one can be a debtor unless others have trusted him. Taxation is also peculiar to civilization, it is the civilized and orderly form of levying contributions for the support of the state; in uncivilized countries rulers exact tribute in any form of value, sometimes even in the form of personal service.

Since, therefore, taxes and debt exist only under conditions which presuppose an organized society and the prevalence of law, we find money invested with the functions of a legal tender only by positive enactment. As the law defines debt and enforces its payment, the law must say what is sufficient payment; as the law levies taxes and requires them to be paid in money, the law must instruct the citizen as to what the medium of payment is to be.*

It is evident that popular confidence and consent are not in any degree necessary to the support of a legal-tender currency. Within its sphere of discharging debts and satisfying the demands of the government, a legal-tender currency exists by force of law alone.

Putting together the results of our inquiries up to this point, we get this definition:

Money is a conventionally recognized and generally accepted medium of exchange and measure of value; it is also, by force of law, a medium for the settlement of contracts and debts, and for the discharge of public dues.

Our money consists of gold coins, gold certificates, silver coins, silver certificates, United States notes (greenbacks), coin notes, and National Bank notes. A given amount in any one of these dif-

---

* It is not necessary that the same form of money shall be prescribed in both cases. A government may make one thing receivable in payment of taxes, and quite another thing legal tender in payment of debt. Thus, until 1878, only gold coins or gold certificates were receivable in payment of duties on imports in the United States, while United States notes have always been legal tender for all debts, and National Bank notes are legal tender only for debts to any National Bank.

ferent kinds of money is precisely equivalent to the same amount in every one of the other kinds, so far as concerns power to buy, to hire, or to command gratifications. While equal in money force, however, these different currencies are very unlike in what is called intrinsic value, which is the value of the material of which they consist, apart from the money character imparted to each by coinage or otherwise.

We all know that the gold in an eagle is worth more than the silver in ten standard dollars, and much more than that in twenty half-dollars, forty quarters, etc., while bank-notes and greenbacks have but little intrinsic value, yet it is a matter of daily experience that ten dollars in one of these forms is precisely equivalent, for the ordinary purposes of money, to the same sum in any other form; that is, all our dollars are of equal money force.

Up to 1888 there was a notable exception to this uniformity of value among dollars. The trade dollar, then existing by authority of our coinage laws, would not buy as much as a standard dollar, nor as much as two halves, four quarters, or ten dimes, although it contained more silver than those, and therefore must have been intrinsically more valuable. Trade dollars did not circulate as money, they did not pass, hence they were not money, but commodities, like medals or silver ornaments. It is the same now with foreign money. Mexican dollars are intrinsically more valuable than ours, but since they do not pass here, they are not money among us. Foreign gold and silver coins, Bank of England notes, etc., though of undoubted value are "uncurrent." It is evident, therefore, that money depends for its force as a medium of exchange and a measure of value upon something besides its form and the quantity and kind of material out of which it is made, and that the character of money is not conferred upon a coin by intrinsic value only, nor upon a note or bill by fully secured representative value, but coins and notes and bills become money only when invested with that character by some power competent to give them general currency in the community.

The next inquiry is, what is the source of the power to command persons and things that distinguishes money from other objects possessing value? The answer is, the source of this power is threefold: First, there is the industrial energy of the age, already described, which compels every one to get money, as the only means whereby he may acquire what he needs or desires. Secondly, there is debt, which forces every debtor to obtain money wherewith to discharge both interest and principal; and thirdly, there is taxation, which compels every taxpayer to procure money for payment into some treasury. These needs for money, one or all, are felt by every one, hence no one can afford not to procure money at every opportunity, whether it be by giving services, by trading, or by selling what he produces.

Since money alone is universally accepted in exchange for whatever is to be disposed of, everybody knows that it is with money alone that he may buy what he likes, hence he will accept only money for what he has to sell, and since the need to sell is quite as coercive as the need to buy, he who has money may command anything that is for sale. So, too, the need of being hired is quite as pressing as the need to hire, hence money commands services as well as things.

The compulsion of taxation and of debt applies almost universally, so that the industrial need of money, imperative of itself, is augmented by the pressure of taxation, and by the incessant accretion of interest. So universal are these forces, compelling men in all conditions of life to obtain money, that there is a universal demand for it, and he who has it possesses a wide choice as to how he shall spend it, while neither property nor commodities, services nor the creations of intellect, can procure desired objects unless first parted with for money.

CHAPTER IV.

NATURAL BASIS OF MONEY

In the preceding chapter money was shown to have certain well-defined functions, of which some rest upon conventional assent and acceptance and others result from the operation of statute law. We shall see hereafter what is the scope and limit of the legal-tender force with which money is endowed by law, also how and why such force is necessary under our present social and industrial conditions.

It is, however, with the more ancient and universal force of money that we are at present concerned, that force by which it had been serving as a medium of exchange and a measure of value for centuries before social and industrial conditions in any part of the world either required or suggested the existence of a legal tender. In investigating the natural force of money, as developed in the performance of those natural functions, we may begin by inquiring in what way it comes about that there is such a thing as money at all, and how the assent and acceptance of the people confer upon it the power to perform its peculiar and important functions.

Money is an indigenous growth of human society, arising out of the needs of mankind.* The inventive faculty of the race contrived the use of money in trade, just as it contrived the use of wheels in transportation. Both contrivances have been developed from rude beginnings into the perfect servants of specialized industry that they are to-day. The development of money seems to have proceeded slowly at first, under no impulse but that of urgent need, and according to no method but what arose out of attrition and the demands of trade. For ages different forms of money prevailed in different parts of the world with but little change, and it is only in comparatively modern times that these forms have been improved by the intelligent application of observation and experience, and that all races and nations have come into harmony as to the substance and form of their money.

While this statement possesses no novelty, it is introduced here because it underlies the only true doctrine of money, and because imaginings to the contrary have led some good men astray, and are still tending to produce errors in our legislation.

What history tells us about the beginning and growth of money is very meagre and very vague, but such as it is, it goes to show that the use of money is an unfailing sign of the presence of some

* Aristotle says: "The use of money was from necessity devised;" and again, "devised from the necessity of mutual exchange."

degree of civilization, and that as civilization has progressed money has become more definite in form and each form more precise and constant in value. Numerous substances have served as money at different times and in different places, which shows that the need of money was felt and that efforts were made to supply that need before the qualities of any particular substance, such as gold or silver, suggested the idea of that substance being made into money.*

It seems to be a law of human development that advancing communities must grope in the dark a long time before they find precisely what they are looking for, whether it be in government, in morals, or in social conveniences; they must try many unfit things before they get what is most fit for their purpose.

The expedients resorted to in primitive social conditions for supplying that need, which we now

* There are persons who imagine, without a shadow of historic authority for it, that mankind, finding gold and silver in the earth, and being impressed with the beauty, the durability, and the divisibility of these metals, began to cast about for uses to which they might be applied, and among other things hit upon the idea of using them for money. Now the fact is, the need of money was felt before gold and silver became applicable to its satisfaction, and this need was supplied by the use of other substances, not only in places where these metals were unknown, but also in places where they abounded. History is full of evidence that in remote antiquity gold and silver were esteemed for their beauty, and were made into ornaments, household utensils, and vessels consecrated to religious uses, but the evidence as to the employment at that time of either of them as money is very questionable.

recognize as a need for money, were only different forms in which men differently situated tried to materialize one and the same idea.

The idea was the same everywhere, because the need was essentially the same everywhere, and the differences among the many forms in which this common idea became embodied resulted from varying limitations of knowledge, or from differences of social condition or of geographical situation, and most frequently, probably, from the irregular occurrence of natural substances suitable for use as money. The idea which found expression in money was begotten of the need of having a medium of exchange, something that would be generally valued alike by everybody, and the first use of money must have been to facilitate barter, because barter was the only method of exchange or trade known, or even practicable, before money came into general use.*

Money was probably at the very first used only as a make-weight in bartering and trading; the "boot," as we call it now. It may be imagined that when bartering and "trading" became close,

---

* Barter is the direct exchange of one commodity for another—a horse for a suit of armor, a yoke of oxen for a piece of land, a sheep for a spear or a sword. It is limited to two persons, and involves a double appraisement by each. Each appraises what he offers and what is offered to him in exchange for it.

This form of trading is still practised, to some extent, as in "swapping horses," etc., and its antiquity is shown by the fact that such a transaction is to this day, in common speech, called by the distinctive appellation of "a trade."

some article of general acceptability was added to the less valuable of the two things under exchange, so as to equalize the values received by the parties to the barter. Naturally the best substance for this would be one in general use and easily divisible without loss of value, and also of rare occurrence as a natural product, hence salt, an article of universal consumption; iron, the material of weapons; copper, the material of armor; silver, the material of household utensils, of personal ornament, and of religious vessels; gold, the material of royal and female adornment, came into use as makeweights or "boot." All these must have had a value of their own in barter;* they were all capable of subdivision by weight; they were wanted everywhere; hence they would be naturally resorted to in order to facilitate or promote other transactions by "evening up" the two sides of the "trade."

It was probably a long time before this primitive stage was passed, but at length men must have perceived that if money could stand for a part of the value of a thing, it could stand for its whole value, and thus money in one or the other of its primitive forms came to be a measure of value, the particular form in each case being determined by the two factors of accessibility and acceptability (supply and demand) at the place of use. The use

---

* John Law appears to have originated the idea that articles used as money must have had a value in barter, but he did not see further how this value became a measure of value.

of money in trade or barter was probably confined for ages to bazaars, fairs, and great assemblies, like those of the Olympic and Isthmian games, where merchants carried it, employed it in their traffic, and no doubt eventually got most of it back again, after it had made the rounds in settling trades all over the place.

That the use of money was thus slowly and gradually evolved may be inferred as a corollary from the proposition that the function of money is to serve as a medium of exchange and a measure of value. This proposition presupposes a stock of exchangeable things, but manifestly in primitive states of society, where industry is as yet undeveloped, and very little of it at all specialized, the stock of such things is small, and therefore the scope of such a medium would be extremely limited; hence, also, conversely, money would be in too limited demand to become generally current. It is probable, therefore, that money came more and more into use and gradually increased in volume, and in the value of the material employed, only as each community progressed in civilization, whereby both the wants and the productions of individuals became diversified. As the volume of money expanded, under the influence of the expanding use for it, its circulation became more rapid, for the greater activity in trade would, of course, require more and more frequently the intervention of a medium of exchange.

The activity of traffic, increasing from century to

century, afforded more frequent opportunities and more numerous inducements to employ money advantageously until, amid the countless industries and dealings of our day, it moves in a million circuits, of which the axes traverse the plane of society in every direction, and cross each other at a thousand points. During the period of this development, from the point at which money was first thrown in as "boot" to close a "trade," down to the point at which we now find it, it gradually came also to be regarded as a measure of value. The origin and growth of this use of money conformed to the natural law of social development, and everywhere history shows a progression of some sort as to the substance used for money, considered as a measure of value.

In every country, and in every race, there was a similar progression, beginning with rude materials of low intrinsic value, and advancing toward finer materials of higher intrinsic value.* Only a natural law could have produced so remarkable a uniformity as history records in the monetary progress of mankind. The same features, the same

* The old Latin term "pecunia" is generally accepted as evidence that, in the infancy of that language, cattle served as money. Afterward, among the same people, the metals came into use, iron first, tin in some places, then copper, then silver, and lastly gold.

"Moneta," from which our term money comes, was of much later origin, and signifies coined or artificial money, as distinguished from what we may call natural money.

The French language, in its two words "l'argent" and "la monnaie," preserves this distinction.

sequences, are repeated over and over again in widely separated communities, cut off from intercourse with one another, and subjected to very widely differing influences, due to their several locations, necessities, and opportunities.

There must, therefore, be a natural law governing this progression; a natural law which tends always to establish as the standard of value the material of highest intrinsic value available at the time.* If there is such a natural law, it must be still operative, and to its effect we may attribute the steadfast movement of modern nations toward silver as the general standard of value, when copper ceased to be adequate, and now toward gold, when silver is no longer adequate.

* We shall see hereafter how such availability depends necessarily upon range of demand.

CHAPTER V.

INDUSTRIAL BASIS OF MONEY

Money being an invention of mankind, perfected by experience and skill, its universal use at the present day results from the universality of industry, and, in turn, modern industry depends for its daily and hourly life upon the uninterrupted circulation of money. Whatever, therefore, may have been the origin of money; whatever function it may have had in the distant past, or in lands where industry is languid, its present use and function among us are matters of such paramount interest and importance that beside them historical inquiries are insignificant.

The people of the United States live mainly by diversified industry; each form of industry depends for existence upon exchanging its products for the products of other forms of industry, and money supplies the only medium of exchange that has so far been found at all adequate to the vital need of sustaining incessant production on the one hand, and supplying incessant consumption on the other. Trade exchanges one product of industry for another, as barter does; but in barter this exchange is direct; in trade it is effected by a process more or less circuitous. Labor is given for money, then the money is given for food. The labor in that way becomes eventually exchanged for food, but only through the use of money. The seller of the food may give the money for other labor, then the first laborer and the second laborer have exchanged their labor, one with another, but since that exchange has been effected by money, neither knows of the exchange so brought about, and neither bestows any thought upon it. Each is interested only, first, in getting as much money as he can for his labor, and secondly, in buying all he can with the money, *i.e.*, making it "go as far as possible."

Without money trade could never have expanded beyond the limits of barter; without trade, industry could never have become specialized; that which has been called (clumsily enough) the division of labor, could never have taken place. Industry, therefore, depends upon money as a medium for the exchange of its diverse products, and at the present day, in civilized countries, money is assisted in this office by credit in various forms. The use of money as a medium of exchange of the products of industry, brings into play also its functions as a measure of value.

The laborer gets a dollar for ten hours' labor, and spends it at his grocer's; the grocer pays this dollar, with another, making two dollars, to his clerk for ten hours' services. Here the laborer has given ten hours' labor for exactly what the clerk earns by five hours' labor, showing that the clerk's labor is worth just twice as much as the laborer's. The dollar, in passing from one of these two men to the other, has measured the value of their labor, and although neither may know that the identical dollar that came from one went to the other, yet, as all dollars are of equal value, each knows full well how his labor compares in value with that of the other. Then, also, each knows how his labor compares in value with the things for sale in the grocery; one knows what he can buy there for a whole day's labor, the other knows that he can buy precisely the same things for a half-day's labor. This knowledge guides each of these men in his contracts for hire, and in his scale of living, while similar knowledge guides all other men, not only in their earnings and expenses, but in all their trading and dealing. Every transaction involves an estimation and a comparison of values.

Value is a relation, and more than that, it is a compound relation. It is the relation between a human desire and the object of that desire on the one hand, and on the other, it is a relation between that object and the desire of its possessor with respect to it.

At every point throughout the industrial world the opposing desires and opinions of buyers and sellers, the conflict of interests and purposes as to the disposition and value of labor services and commodities, create an incessant contention, out of which, and by means of which, definite results as to value are obtained, and these results are expressed under the designation of price, in denominations of money. The prices of wheat, cotton, iron, tobacco, petroleum, etc., are established in this way; each article fluctuates in price as the buyers or the sellers of it preponderate in effective force, and these in turn are influenced in their estimates of value and in pertinacity of opinion by their knowledge, or by what they suppose to be their knowledge, or, perhaps, simply by their guesses, as to the relation between the supply of, and the demand for, the particular article in which they deal.

Prices are always expressed in money, and values are estimated in money, hence we are accustomed to regard price and value as identical, but they are not so, for price is only the exponent of estimated value.

The price of an article comes nearest to its value when it reflects an appraisement established by the concurrence of buyers and sellers; but as this concurrence is effected only by incessant conflict and contention, the point of ultimate concurrence varies incessantly, while values change less frequently; hence the price of a commodity may fluctuate daily, while its changes of value would about conform to the mean of these daily fluctuations.

Since money is ordinarily the only measure of value generally accessible, since trade depends at every turn upon measuring values in order to compare them, and since a comparison of values is essential to the exchange of the products of industry, and since, finally, industry, diversified and specialized as it is among us, exists from day to day, even from hour to hour, only by means of an exchange of products based upon relative values, it follows necessarily that industry, and all who live by industry, have a vital interest in money regarded as a measure of value. They depend upon it absolutely.

Now, whatever is depended upon as a measure of anything, must itself be constant and unchanging in respect to the quality which it is to measure. A measure of length must not be subject to linear contraction and expansion; a measure of weight must not be subject to changes in its own weight; a measure of time must be chronometrically accurate; a measure of force must never show variable results under identical conditions; hence money, as a measure of value, should itself be free from variation in value.* Money that fluctuates in value misleads those who depend upon it to measure other values, themselves fluctuating, and since all persons engaged in productive and commercial industry, all who buy and all who sell, must incessantly depend upon using money as a measure

* In speaking here of the value of money, what is meant is the intrinsic or conventional value of the coins or notes which constitute the money of any given community. In the financial articles of newspapers, the term value of money is habitually used to express the rate of interest for loans. This, of course, is quite another matter.

and gauge of fluctuating values, it follows that all such persons are misled, to their injury, when money is not fixed in its own value.

To sum up this chapter, it may be said that industry depends upon money as a medium of exchange; that to serve this purpose, money must be also a measure of value, and that as a measure of value it should be itself unchangeable in value. Unless these conditions exist, industry will become disordered, and all persons will suffer who are dependent upon industry; which means, practically, all the people of the United States.

CHAPTER VI.

LAW AS A BASIS OF MONEY

We have now ascertained the ordinary functions of money; we have seen that its use arose by force of natural laws, as the use of wheels and the use of language arose; that industry is dependent upon it, both as a medium of exchange and as a measure of value, and that to serve these purposes money must itself be first definite in value, and, moreover, unchangeable in value. Manifestly, the next point to be considered is, how is money invested with a definite value, and then how is that value preserved against change?

Definiteness of value depends upon definiteness of material and form; permanency of value depends upon continuous, intelligent regulation as to material and form. These things can be accomplished in the highest degree only by law; not natural law alone, because natural law merely supplies general principles; the practical application of these principles to the purposes of society must be accomplished by human law—the excellence of the human laws affecting money being, however, always proportioned to the degree in which they conform to the principles of natural law.

In communities where society has not yet reached a degree of development which brings it under settled government and written law, local conditions and ideas bring about, in process of time, a general concensus of the people as to the form and value of the money best suited to their use, and what is thus evolved is afterward maintained by custom; but when government is perfected these matters are more fully provided for by law. Deferring for the present all consideration of the constitutional and statutory sanction enjoyed by the money we use, let us look at the genesis of the relation between money and the law.*

In the progress of society from barbarism to civilization, and while government was being developed from its rude beginning in patriarchal or military chieftainship into what it is to-day in the most advanced countries of the world, a highly organized institution, recognizing the varied interests of the community and providing for the general welfare of the people—in the course of this development what were once prerogatives of the sovereign, arbitrarily exercised, have been

---

* Money was in use before there were any laws concerning it, hence the first edicts on the subject must have recognized whatever money was then and there current, thus establishing the proposition that in respect to money the function of civil law is to accept, preserve, and apply the principles disclosed by the operation of natural laws. The earliest laws on this subject, of which there is any record, related to money measures or to coinages already in general use, and history shows that the regulation of money has always been regarded as one of the prerogatives of sovereignty.

from time to time limited and defined by law or revolution, so that they are now obligatory functions of the state, and government has been constantly enlarging the sphere of its activity and increasing the number of its functions.

One of the duties thus devolved upon modern government is that of selecting the material of money, prescribing its forms, and fixing its value, and it is in this way, and under these conditions that law is a basis of our money. If the law did not prescribe the material and form of our money; if the law did not establish a monetary unit for measuring values, we should have to seek these through some other means less effectual for the purpose, and it should be observed that this statement is not inconsistent with the doctrine that money has its primary basis in natural laws, and that it has existed and may exist independently of any statute, edict, or decree emanating from civil authority.

Although it may at first seem superfluous for the law to concern itself with what existed before there were law-governed communities, and what would continue to exist if there were neither parliaments nor congresses, mints nor public treasuries, it is not so. Roads, bridges, and ferries have been constructed and used before there were laws providing for their establishment and maintenance, but civilization requires that in populous communities these should be provided and regulated by the public authority. So it is with money.

That which suffices for barbarous nations would not satisfy those that are civilized, and in our day the uses of money are much more important and diversified than they have ever been before.

It is obvious that as respects taxes and debts there must be some medium of payment prescribed by the law that imposes the one and sanctions the other, for since the law undertakes to enforce payment in these cases the law alone can fix what shall constitute such payment. But, one may ask, why should the law presume to say what I must take in payment for my labor, my talents, my property, or my land? Why should I not be free to dispose of these as I like, as is done where only natural law prevails? The answer to this is, that every one is free to do so, but since ordinarily none exercise that freedom because it is more convenient to accept the money the government provides, there is no stock of any other money in the community.*

It may be thought hastily that one need not dispose of his labor, etc., at all unless he is satisfied with the money provided by law, but this is not true in a practical sense, in our day and country. Here he who lives by daily employment is absolutely dependent upon disposing of his labor, or the products of his brain, day by day. If one

---

* In countries where there are no bridges travellers generally find roads leading to fords, but when the bridge is built these roads cease to be used and become obliterated and thereafter travellers must use the bridge.

is a trader, and has his capital in goods, he must sell to keep his customers and to realize the profits necessary to his support. The farmer must sell such of his products as he cannot use, in order to buy the things he needs but does not himself produce; the manufacturer must dispose of his products in order to pay the hands and keep the machinery running; in a word, industry renders the great mass of the people dependent upon the use of money from day to day, even from hour to hour; hence whatever money the government provides must be used by all, whether they like it or not.

In a later chapter we shall see that when men do not like the money in use, when they do not trust it, that very opinion inflicts loss upon them by causing the money to depreciate on their hands. Every effort that each individual makes to avoid taking it, or when that cannot be accomplished to pass it off as quickly as possible upon someone else, aggravates the depreciation. It will also appear that individuals, either singly or when voluntarily combined in numbers less than the whole population, are powerless to stay the tide of general distrust; it is unsafe for one or many to trust a currency that is not equally trusted by all; when the whole army is retreating, the single soldier, regiment, or brigade that tries to stand its ground encounters certain destruction, without glory and without benefit to the common cause.

Since, therefore, the people individually, or

even by voluntary combination in large numbers, cannot sustain a currency not universally trusted, it is evident that in order to command general confidence the value of the money in use must be vouched for by some authority universally known and respected, and in modern nations the government is such an authority, and it vouches for the money by subjecting its coinage or manufacture to the regulation of law.

This is the basis in reason for the control of law over money, and our laws on this subject have a historical basis and constitutional sanction entirely consonant with this view. During our colonial days, and during the period between the establishment of the independence of the United States and the adoption of the present Constitution, the people of the country, as a whole, were without any constituted authority empowered to exercise this function, and they suffered great and manifold evils in consequence. Under the influence of this experience the framers of the Constitution vested in Congress "the power to coin money, regulate the value thereof, and of foreign coins, and fix the standard of weights and measures."

Another clause provides that "no State shall coin money, emit bills of credit, or make anything but gold and silver coins a tender in payment of debts."

These two clauses of the Constitution vest in the United States Government exclusive control over the money of the people, and since, as has been proved, such control should be lodged somewhere, it is eminently proper that it should be lodged where the people themselves can prescribe how it shall be exercised. The wise fathers of the Constitution were familiar, not only with the experiences of their own times, and of the generations immediately before them, but they had looked into the pages of history and had learned there how the people of all ages and all parts of the world had suffered from the abuse of this power by their arbitrary rulers.*

That the control of the material, the forms, and the value of their money, should be retained in the hands of the people collectively, who, as individuals, depend upon it so constantly and so vitally, seems an ideal realization of the fundamental principle of the natural laws we have been heretofore considering, and it is interesting to reflect that the long process of development, beginning in prehistoric times, and passing through so many ages, nations, and social phases, should have attained in our day and country its natural culmination in placing in the hands of the people the power to coin their own money and to regulate its value.

The Constitution, however, prescribes that this power shall be exercised by the people through their representatives in Congress, and whether constitutionally or otherwise, Congress has placed a very wide construction upon this grant of power, hence it behooves the people to know what limita-

* See Adam Smith. Wealth of Nations, Book V., chap. iii., p. 396. London: T. Nelson & Sons, 1865.

tions are imposed upon its exercise by the natural laws on which the constitutional grant is founded, and by which, therefore, it should be interpreted.

This inquiry is momentous in practical importance, because unless Congress exercises its powers in conformity with natural laws, there will inevitably arise a state of things contravening those laws, and such a situation invariably leads to disaster. Nature never fails to assert her supremacy when it is disregarded, and to punish those who ignore her institutes or transgress her laws. Let an architect disregard the natural law of gravity or fail to study or to apply the principles of molecular cohesion; let an engineer misinterpret the natural laws of pneumatics; let a farmer ignore the natural laws of plant-life or of animal nutrition; let a community neglect the natural laws of hygiene, the consequences are certain and disastrous; but they are no more certain, and they are far less disastrous because less wide-spread, than are the consequences that follow upon the ignorant or the wilful contravention by government of the natural laws that control the use of money.

Every departure from true principles in monetary legislation is mischievous because it deranges those delicate adjustments between balanced values that supply the only stable foundation for commercial confidence, whereas commercial confidence being essential to an active trade and to uninterrupted industry is therefore essential to general prosperity.

LAW AS A BASIS OF MONEY

The whole function of government, with respect to money, is limited, first, to establishing by law what shall constitute the general medium of exchange, measure of value, and legal tender for debt and public dues, and, secondly, to protecting this money from variations in value one way or the other. The form and material of the money, the method by which the supply may be adjusted to the needs of the people, the establishment and maintenance of a monetary unit are details requiring the application of knowledge drawn from observation and experience both as to the natural laws which underlie all such things, and as to the condition, the methods, and the necessities of industry in the community over which the monetary system prevails.

Sentiment, prejudices, ignorance, vague and ill-digested theories, experiments and shifting expedients, are pernicious in their effects everywhere and always, but when embodied in monetary laws they work evils hard to detect and harder still to cure; they cast a blight upon industry and sow ruin and demoralization broadcast among the people.

CHAPTER VII.

CONFIDENCE AS A BASIS OF MONEY

All the teachings of history, all the logic of political economy, all the facts of common experience in respect to money, concur in support of the proposition that public confidence can make anything pass as money, and, conversely, that nothing can so pass unless there is confidence in the future continuity of its efficiency as a medium of purchase and payment.

Mistaken confidence, as long as it lasts, is quite as effective for this purpose as confidence sagaciously given, and a mistaken withholding or withdrawal of confidence is just as fatal as that which ensues from right reasoning. Every transition from the use of one currency to that of another has afforded illustrations of the truth of this proposition. We have lately seen silver discredited, and no one can doubt that gold, too, would have its efficiency as money affected if the universal confidence in its future supremacy as a medium of international settlement should be disturbed.

In the United States, as in other countries similarly developed, it is the province of the law to determine the material of money, to prescribe its form or forms, and to fix its value; but the law cannot make it circulate unless the money itself enjoys the confidence of the people.

Whether any particular form of money is or is not entitled to command this confidence will depend wholly upon how the government exercises its prerogative of regulating money, for the conditions determining public confidence in respect to money arise out of natural laws, which are superior in force to statutes. These conditions inevitably limit the free action of every government, and hence they should be respected in all monetary legislation. History establishes it as a fact, that when the material of money is a precious metal, possessing intrinsic value equal to the money force conferred upon the coins by law, when this value is stable, when the coinage laws are not subject to capricious change, when the monetary unit or standard of value is fixed and steadfastly adhered to, such money will command and retain public confidence under all circumstances and in times of the greatest general confusion. Its money value has a natural basis in its intrinsic value.

There is also historical evidence to show that when these conditions are either not all originally present, or have become varied by events, still public confidence in certain forms of money may be won and preserved by the force of the government's credit. In such cases the credit of the government is substituted for the whole or for a part of that intrinsic value which constitutes the natural basis of money, and the degree of confidence thus imparted to any particular form of money depends, of course, upon the degree of the government's credit.

The correlative of credit is confidence; to obtain credit one must enjoy the confidence of those from whom it is to be obtained, and hence, when a government appeals to its people, or to others, to extend to its money credit, as a substitute, wholly or in part, for intrinsic value in the money itself, that government must be prepared to show that it is entitled to their confidence and determined to continue to merit it. Confidence cannot be exacted; like affection, respect, and gratitude, it must be won, and to be surely won it must be deserved. Even after being thus obtained, confidence can be perpetuated only by conduct meriting its continuance. The fundamental condition, therefore, of popular confidence in any form of money, except coins of full and established intrinsic value, is the credit of the government, which is equivalent to saying that the money force of such currency depends upon trust in the government.

Now, public trust in the government includes three distinct beliefs.

1st. Belief in the good faith of the government; that is, in its purpose to fulfil all obligations expressed and implied in its engagements. This belief is fundamental to all credit, to that of individuals as well as to that of governments, because without such belief confidence could find no solid foundation, and confidence is the state of mind of which the objective manifestation is trust.

2d. Belief in the stability of the government; that is, that it will continue to have the power to apply the national resources to the fulfilment of its engagements.

This, too, is obviously a necessary element in confidence. When the form of government is monarchical, stability means absence of revolution, but when, as with us, the government is impersonal, stability means something different. A representative and impersonal government is the mere organ of the community, and if there is danger that the community, in changing its organ, may at the same time abrogate and repudiate the engagements then subsisting, the government will not be regarded as the organ of the community for making such engagements, and, therefore, such government may not command that degree of confidence which the personal character and unquestioned good faith of its officers should inspire and which the national wealth justifies. The steward of a wealthy man derives power to use his employer's credit, not from the latter's wealth alone, but from the extent and permanency of his control over that wealth. A precarious stewardship will attract no confidence, and therefore can acquire no credit. Hence, stability, under our form of government, implies a settled purpose among the people to require all public obligations to be fulfilled, however local politics may vary.

3d. Belief in the sufficiency of the material resources of the government for fulfilling its engagements.

It is evident that an individual may be honest and earnestly resolved to perform every contract he makes, that he may have an assured position, a stable business, and good health [qualities in an individual corresponding as nearly as practicable with stability in government], and yet, if his undertakings are suspected to be beyond accomplishment by the means within his reach; if those invited to assist him, upon trust in his future ability to perform, doubt that ability, he will lack a very material element of credit.

So it is with governments; a government that asks to be trusted must vindicate its claim to confidence, first, by establishing a "character," *i.e.*, a reputation for honesty of purpose and integrity, both in legislation and administration; secondly, by satisfying the public as to the permanency of its hold upon the national resources and upon the official machinery for bringing those resources under its control in the discharge of its obligations; but, beyond both these requirements, there is the further indispensable condition that the national resources at the disposal of the government shall be sufficient to the discharge of such obligations, not only ultimately, but when the obligations mature.

These three elements, therefore, constitute the substance of government credit, and when they all exist in the highest degree, that credit is generally sufficient to support a portion at least of the monetary circulation.

There is, however, something else wanting to the complete monetary efficiency of any form of money that depends wholly or partially upon government credit, and that is, its convertibility into other money that derives its value wholly from intrinsic qualities.

Since, at the present time, greenbacks and gold certificates enjoy equal confidence, though the coin basis of the greenbacks is only about thirty per cent. of their volume, it may appear that the convertibility of credit money into real money is not necessarily an element of public confidence in the former, but it must be considered that potential convertibility suffices to support confidence until the test of actual conversion fails; what sustains a convertible credit-currency in circulation is the belief that in any particular instance it will stand that test.

It may be perfectly well known, for example, that the government keeps only $100,000,000 in gold with which to redeem $346,000,000 of greenbacks; but as long as the public believe that this sum is sufficient to maintain the convertibility of the entire greenback issue, few, if any, greenbacks will be presented for redemption; while, if confidence upon this point should become disturbed, the $100,000,000 redemption fund would immediately have "a run" made upon it, like the run made by depositors upon a discredited bank. The basis of this confidence is twofold; first, a knowledge that it will take a considerable time to exhaust $100,000,000 by the ordinary processes of redemption; and, secondly, that the resources of the government are ample for repairing any probable drain upon this reserve of coin.

These being the principles underlying that public confidence which is essential to money as an effective servant of society, let us test them by the experience of our own people, and apply them to the circumstances of the present time.

The money existing in the United States during the last dozen years has been of various kinds; gold coins, silver coins, gold certificates, silver certificates, currency certificates, greenbacks, and National Bank notes, to which are now added "coin notes," issued under the act of July, 1890. Since January 1, 1879, it has all enjoyed equal confidence, that is to say, it has all circulated indiscriminately; has been equally effective in purchasing; has been of uniform, and therefore of interchangeable, value.

Before 1879, however, this was not the case; gold coin and gold certificates then were more valuable than corresponding denominations of greenbacks and National Bank notes.* The reason why greenbacks and National Bank notes were less valu-

---

* There were no silver dollars at that time, and the subsidiary coin being of low intrinsic value and used only for change, is not taken note of here or elsewhere in this treatise.

able than gold, before 1879, is because the credit currency did not then stand as high in popular confidence as did gold coins and the gold certificates.

When, however, the government provided for the convertibility of its paper into gold, first, by the Resumption Act, and then by actually getting the gold in hand to effect resumption, the confidence of the people in the greenbacks and National Bank notes rose to the level of their confidence in gold itself. The paper currency came to "par," as the phrase goes.

If we analyze the grounds of this confidence we shall find that it rested on the three distinct beliefs already enumerated, viz.:

1st. Belief in the good faith of the government, *i.e.*, that having promised to redeem this paper in gold the government meant to do so.

2d. Belief in the stability of the government. Of course this does not mean simply belief in the maintenance of the Union and of the Constitution, but belief also in the permanent legislative and administrative supremacy of men pledged and determined to fulfil the public obligations. It may or may not have been a party question, but, in either case, public confidence in this respect necessarily depends upon the public belief that whoever might be the people's representatives they would be required to observe the plighted faith of the government.

3d. Belief in the means of the government for

fulfilling its undertaking to establish and maintain the convertibility of greenbacks into gold.

It will be profitable to follow this instructive episode in our recent monetary experience somewhat in detail.

When the greenbacks, which are the government's due bills, were depreciated, that depreciation was the sign of the government's discredit; the rate of depreciation was the measure of the degree of such discredit. This discredit of the government, before 1879, may have been due to the absence of either of the three beliefs enumerated above as constituting public confidence, or to the absence of any two of them or of all three. That it was not due to the absence of belief in the honesty or in the stability of the government, may be inferred from the fact that the gold certificates issued by the Treasury for gold deposited there were freely accepted as equivalent to the gold itself. This would not have happened if the honesty or the stability of the government had been doubted. Indeed, in that case, there would have been no gold certificates at all, because these are issued only for voluntary deposits of gold, and no one would have deposited gold and taken a certificate for it if he had thought he might not get back gold on demand. It follows, therefore, that the depreciation of the greenbacks before 1875 was due partly to the absence of legislative provision for their redemption, and partly to a doubt as to whether the government could command sufficient means to redeem them in gold on demand, even if Congress should so resolve; while their depreciation between January, 1875, and January, 1879, was due wholly to this doubt.

That this was actually the case is proved by the fact that the Resumption Act, which was passed January 14, 1875,* did not raise the greenbacks to par, but the accumulation of $70,000,000 of gold coin in the Treasury brought the gold premium down, and the negotiation of $50,000,000, of bonds for $50,000,000 of gold coin finally extinguished it. The credit of the government was perfected, not by the law, but by the financial operations

---

* Section 3 of the Resumption Act provides: " . . . it shall be the duty of the Secretary of the Treasury to redeem the legal tender United States notes in excess only of three hundred million of dollars, to the amount of eighty per centum of the sum of National Bank notes so issued to any such banking association as aforesaid, and to continue such redemption as such circulating notes are issued, until there shall be outstanding the sum of three hundred million dollars of such legal tender United States notes, and no more. And on and after the first day of January, Anno Domini eighteen hundred and seventy-nine, the Secretary of the Treasury shall redeem, in coin, the United States legal tender notes then outstanding, on their presentation for redemption at the office of the Assistant Treasurer of the United States in the city of New York, in sums of not less than fifty dollars. And to enable the Secretary of the Treasury to prepare and provide for the redemption in this act authorized or required, he is authorized to use any surplus revenues, from time to time, in the Treasury, not otherwise appropriated, and to issue, sell, and dispose of, at not less than par, in coin, either of the descriptions of bonds of the United States described in the act of Congress approved July fourteenth, eighteen hundred and seventy, entitled 'An Act to authorize the refunding of the national debt.'"

that rendered resumption practicable. This recent event in our experience proves the necessity of all the three elements to the perfection of credit, and it also affords a clear demonstration that the preservation of the convertibility of the greenbacks, and, therefore, of the credit of our government at home, with its own people, depends absolutely upon its credit in the money markets of the world. If that loan of $50,000,000 had been impracticable, the greenbacks would not have gone to par, and the loan was practicable only because the bankers of this country and of Europe believed that the bonds were a safe investment. No one can deny these facts; no one can question this deduction from them.

Now, undoubtedly, the confidence of the foreign bankers who lent the greater part of this $50,000,000 rested upon their belief in the honesty and intelligence, as well as in the resources of the people of the United States, and this emphasizes what must always be the prime consideration in determining the degree of financial credit to which a government like ours is entitled, namely, the intelligence, the knowledge, the experience, and the sense of responsibility attributed to those who are in a position to control its financial legislation and administration.

In private life the credit enjoyed by a merchant depends, in a great degree, upon his general business intelligence, his knowledge of the article in which he deals, his experience in that particular trade, the character of his partners and agents, and his sensitiveness to the demands of commercial honor, because those are essential to his success in business, and credit cannot exist unless there is confidence in the debtor's means to command success in every way and permanently. In like manner the credit of a government largely depends upon confidence in the qualifications of the persons entrusted with the management, of its finances, and in a popular government like ours, regard will also be had to the prevalence among the people generally of sound monetary doctrines. While it is true that of all governments one directly responsible to a people engrossed in industry is under the highest obligations to cherish and maintain the national credit, yet it is also true that these obligations are but little understood, and that the people of the United States, through their representatives, can break all contracts and invalidate all bonds, while no physical power on earth could coerce the payment of either the principal or interest of the national debt if Congress should refuse, or even should omit to provide for such payment.

The bonds of such a government may seem but slight security for $50,000,000 of gold coin; but the bankers who took our bonds in 1878 knew that the natural laws of finance gave them a grip upon the people of the United States more sure and more durable than could be secured by the combined fleets and armies of Europe. These natural laws compel every commercial people to sustain the national credit at any sacrifice, and under all circumstances, on peril of intolerable loss. The repudiation of those bonds would cost the people of the United States vastly more than they would gain by extinguishing the debt of $50,000,000 in that way; it would cost us not less than six times as much, while the mere attempt to repudiate, even if afterward abandoned, would cost us eventually more than $50,000,000.

Can this be doubted? Consider the effect of discrediting the government of the United States. Remember we ourselves, *i.e.*, the masses of the people, did not credit it for the full face value of a single greenback of the $340,000,000 then outstanding until after the bankers, foreign and domestic, had agreed to lend it $50,000,000 of gold to be added to $70,000,000 already hoarded in the Treasury. When this immense sum of gold was in sight, and we had, moreover, a law authorizing and requiring the Secretary of the Treasury to sell more bonds for the special purpose of redeeming the greenbacks, and when, moreover, it was obvious that there was still a market for further issues of bonds, then, and not until then, did we venture fully to trust our own government. Now let the government lose its credit with the bankers, can it be retained among the people? Surely not. The $100,000,000 of gold now held as a special redemption fund will be drawn out as fast as greenbacks can be handed in through every aperture of the redemption counters of the Treasury, and then there will remain $246,000,000 of greenbacks in the hands of the people, and neither gold to redeem them with nor credit with which to get more gold. These will, of course, immediately depreciate, how much is immaterial to our immediate purpose; let us say, only ten per cent. That will take ten per cent. off the purchasing power of $378,000,000 of silver dollars, $246,000,000 of greenbacks, about $172,000,000 of National Bank notes [because they are redeemable in greenbacks], making $796,000,000 of currency, on which ten per cent. is $79,600,000.

In the last report of the Comptroller of the Currency (December, 1892), deposits of all the State banks and trust companies are estimated at $1,060,-000,000; savings bank deposits, $1,760,000,000; individual deposits in National Banks, $1,780,000,-000; private bankers deposits, $90,000,000. Total debt of the banks, etc., to the people, payable in lawful money, $4,690,000,000. These deposits would of course follow the value of the lawful money in which they are payable. If that should be depreciated ten per cent., every depositor will lose ten cents on the dollar in the real value—the purchasing power—of whatever amount he has on deposit.

On the $4,690,000,000 of deposits above shown, the loss would be $469,000,000; and the loss on currency, as above, would be $79,600,000; aggregate loss on above items resulting from ten per cent. depreciation of greenbacks, $548,600,000. Here, then, is the sword held over us. Here is the power that compels us to preserve the credit of our government; that is, not to shake the confidence of capitalists and bankers at home or abroad in the honesty of our people, and the intelligence and the prudence of our national legislators. But if we find in these considerations the most insuperable obstacle to countenancing any act that may cause such loss to our people by its mere recoil, how much more reason do they afford for not only discountenancing but denouncing and strenuously preventing any legislation that, while respecting our obligations to bankers and foreigners, nevertheless impairs the credit of the government among its own people, and through debasing the standard by which their money is valued inflicts upon them losses of stupendous magnitude.

Our circulation now includes: Greenbacks about $346,000,000; National Bank notes, $172,000,000; silver dollars and silver and coin certificates, say $492,000,000; making the total of paper and silver held up to a parity of value with gold by the credit of the government, $1,016,000,000.

The entire value of the greenbacks and National Bank notes depends upon credit, while the silver dollars and silver certificates derive more than a fourth of their value from credit. Impair that credit, and for every one per cent. of currency depreciation resulting from its impairment, you will inflict upon the people who are holding the currency, a loss of $10,760,000; and upon depositors in banks, etc., $46,900,000; here is a loss, for every one per cent. depreciation of $57,660,000. If the currency drops to the intrinsic value of 412½ grains of silver to the dollar, now 65 cents, that will be a loss of over thirty-five per cent., or more than $2,000,000,000, which is more than three times the entire volume of the national bonded debt still unpaid.

Who can doubt that this result will follow upon any act of our government which lets go the gold standard? It cannot be denied that we must have a solid metallic basis of value somewhere for our currency. When a paper promise to pay ten dollars is presented to the promisor for redemption, there must be some real intrinsic value handed over in fulfilment of the promise. What is it to be? According to existing laws it must be coins containing either 258 grains of gold, or else 4.125 grains of silver 900 fine. There is no standard but these two by which to measure ten dollars in this country, and as these two standards differ in real value, the time will come when we must cleave to the one and forsake the other.

Admit, for the sake of argument merely, that the government can elect to make the silver dollar the standard; dare we encounter the consequences? At present, the standard is gold—gold by force of the statute of February 12, 1873, establishing the dollar of 25.8 grains of gold, nine-tenths fine, as the monetary unit; gold by contract under the Resumption Act of 1875; gold according to the real worth of the $4,690,000,000 of good money lent by the people to the banks, in the form of deposits, and now owed by the banks to the people in gold; gold by the common understanding and business dealings of the people during the last twenty years. State, municipal, railroad and other corporation bonds, private bonds, notes and contracts, salaries, wages, rents and taxes, are all on a gold basis, placed there in consequence of the popular faith in these solemn enactments by Congress, sanctioned by public acquiescence.

Let Congress say, now, that the standard is the silver dollar, and straightway a loss of $1,260,000,-000 will fall upon those among the people of the United States who have no gold, no foreign exchange, no government bonds, no bank stock.

The people, the masses, who have deposits in the various banks, and who hold the money provided by the government, will have to bear the entire loss. What boots it that a large part of this fearful loss will be offset by gains to those [banks and bankers] who now owe this money, and who have been wise enough or fortunate enough to invest it abroad, or to hold it here in gold, or in securities convertible into gold? No man who is a loser suffers less because another man gains by his loss. If the many were to be gainers and the few to be losers there is a sort of political conscience that might be easy under responsibility for legislation effecting that result; but here the case is reversed; there will be a hundred thousand losers for every ten possible gainers. Again, if the poor, as a class, were to be the gainers, and the rich, as a class, the losers, there is another sort of politico-socialistic conscience that might approve, but in the case supposed the reverse will take place; the poor will all be made poorer, the great bulk of the people who are in moderate circumstances will bear the chief loss, while some few among the rich may possibly be made richer. If these things are clearly apprehended, either in Congress or among the people, will any voice be raised to disturb the public confidence now enjoyed by our money? No patriot, no statesman could wish to disturb it; no demagogue or fanatic would dare to do so.

Yet these things must be true, because they are the result of principles as fundamental to social life and industry as are the principles of gravity and cohesion to physical existence. Sooner or later they will be universally recognized, because, if we do not apprehend them through our intelligence, they will impress themselves forcibly upon our sensation. The man who ignores gravity falls and suffers pain; the nation that ignores the natural laws of finance invokes disaster and will inevitably suffer it.

CHAPTER VIII.

DEFINITENESS AND STABILITY OF VALUE THE SOLE ESSENTIAL QUALITIES OF MONEY

We have seen that money had its origin in the development of society from primitive conditions into civilization, and that at the present day its bases are to be found in industry, in law, and in the confidence of the people. So far, our investigations have been confined to the conditions under which money is used; we now come to the money itself. What quality must money possess in order to conform to natural law, to serve the needs of industry, to command the confidence by which alone it can fulfil its functions as a medium of exchange and a measure of value, and hence to merit the sanction of civil law?

The answer is, the qualities essentially requisite for money are, definiteness and stability of value; that is, a dollar, a franc, or a shilling must have a settled definite value, and this value should be guarded against change. This may be made plain by means of an illustration already used, in which money was represented as an order in favor of its possessor for such form of value as he may desire. Manifestly, the first requisite in any order is that it should be definite in its terms. If one acquires for value a delivery order for goods, he requires it to specify the quantity or the weight which he is to receive, and these are expressed in yards or pounds or perhaps tons. This is definite enough, provided there is an accurate understanding and agreement among all parties concerned as to the standard of measurement or of weight which is to govern the transaction.

This definiteness and this agreement is so essential to all such transactions that every civilized government has established by law, standards of weights and measures which are immutable, while the laws require contracts to be settled by the standards appropriate to the measurement of the article concerned. Without such standards and laws, orders and contracts for the delivery of commodities could not be dealt in at all. Now, money is an order for value; the material substance to be delivered depends upon the will of the holder of the order, who is limited in his choice only by the supply of desired articles, but whatever obtainable article may be selected will have its value settled by the amount of money given for it. A dollar is an order for a dollar's worth of labor, of cloth, of food, etc.; of course the holder must take it to the proper dealer, since he cannot get labor from his butcher, nor cloth from his gardener, but to whomsoever he takes it from that dealer he is entitled to full value—a dollar's worth. Now it is manifest that a standard of value, fixed and immutable, is just as necessary to the circulation of money as is a standard of weights and measures to the passing of orders for goods.* He who gives labor for a dollar wants to be absolutely sure that that dollar will have, in his hands, the power to command as much value as he gave for it in labor. It is not really the dollar that is worked for, but it is the dollar's worth of things wanted. Hence the degree of value which is expressed by the term "dollar" should be fixed and definite, for, without such fixed and definite value, the dollar cannot be used in comparing values, nor can it be used in exchanging them without involving incessant reappraisements of the dollar itself.

Men desire to exchange and to compare values every time a contract is made for wages, services, rent, etc., and every time a commodity or any kind of property is being bargained for. In the payment of wages, and in all small transactions, the current money of the time and place is used to measure values, just as in the retail trade the yard-stick is used to measure cloth, pound weights to measure sugar, or pint cups to measure molasses. But beyond the retail trade goods are passed from hand to hand among whole-

* In the United States Constitution the two stand in juxtaposition — coinage and the regulation of weights and measures (Article I. Section VIII.); and this close association has been preserved in the designation of one of the Standing Committees of the House of Representatives "On Coinage, Weights, and Measures."

sale dealers by the package or bale, the barrel or hogshead, and are paid for by checks or drafts.*

In the export and import trade the ownership of cargoes passes upon delivery of bills of lading; payment is made for the quantities specified in the invoices of the seller, and such payment is by bill of exchange. Now the packages, bales, barrels, hogsheads, and cargoes are aggregations of quantity and weight, based upon primary and fixed units of weight and measurement; in like manner amounts of dollars or pounds sterling, specified in checks, drafts, and bills of exchange, are aggregations of money based upon a primary and fixed unit of value, designated by the term dollar or the term pound sterling. Hence, as the legal ounce is the primary unit or standard of weight for cargoes sold by the thousands of tons, so the legal dollar or pound sterling is the monetary unit or standard of value for the check, draft, or bill of exchange which pays for the cargo.

The selling of goods in large quantities, by aggregated weights and measures, is an economy in time, and so, also, the payments of large sums, by checks or drafts, is an economy of time. If it were not for these modes of aggregating quantity on the one hand, and aggregating value on the other, much time would necessarily be consumed in measuring or weighing the contents of

* Bonds and stocks are paid for in the same way.

cargoes and in counting out coins to the amount of the draft or check.*

Beyond all considerations of convenience and economy there is underlying both the handling of quantities of commodities in packages, cargoes, etc., and the massing of value into checks and drafts, a necessity that there should be a fixed unit of weight or measure in the one case, and a fixed unit of value in the other; for without a perfect understanding and agreement between buyer and seller as to the actual weight of an ounce, and the actual value of a dollar, these transactions could never occur; merchants demand this certainty in all their dealings, and they are generally able as well as careful to secure it. If the man who is about paying for a cargo by the thousand tons has any doubt as to what constitutes an ounce in the estimation of the person who has weighed the cargo at the port of shipment, he will not make the payment until he has verified the weight by his own scales; but if there is no doubt upon that point, he pays by the weight specified in the bills of lading.

So if the man to whom payment for this cargo is being made in the form of check or draft, has no doubt as to the real value, *i.e.*, the kind of

---

* Drafts, checks, etc., are aggregated values expressed in money terms and convertible into money upon certain conditions, so that it has become a habit to speak of these aggregations of value as money, whereas they are not money any more than a bill of lading is a cargo of cotton, or the elevator receipt for a thousand bushels of wheat is in reality wheat itself.

DEFINITENESS AND STABILITY OF VALUE 83

dollars, represented by these paper orders for money, he accepts them as if they were money; but if he has doubts, he requires to be assured upon this point before parting with the bills of lading, which are paper orders for his property. The quantity or weight specified in the bills of lading being fixed, he very reasonably demands equal certitude as to the exact value he is to get in exchange. Now, just as the mint mark supplies an assurance as to the weight and fineness of metal in coin, so does the law establishing a monetary unit supply an assurance as to the real value recoverable upon a note, a draft, or a check, payable in dollars. The monetary unit established by law also supplies a standard by which all values may be measured, and their measurement reduced to money terms, just as the unit of linear measure established by law supplies a standard by which the physical extension of all bodies may be measured, and their measurements reduced to terms of linear dimension.

It is absolutely necessary to have a unit of value, not only for measuring values, but for expressing their measurement accurately, because unless the several values of different objects can be thus ascertained by a common unit or value-measure, and unless they can be expressed in terms common to all, these values cannot be compared with the requisite degree of exactness for the purposes of trade and commerce. Without the means for such comparison industry would be paralyzed, because modern industry depends for its maintenance upon incessant interchange of products, and, as we have seen, this interchange proceeds wholly by means of a comparison of the exact values of different commodities, or of similar commodities at different places and times.

The unit of the English money system was formerly the shilling, now it is the pound sterling.* The unit of the French system is the franc; the unit of our system is the dollar. These, however, are mere names and may be applied to anything; they acquire definiteness as terms expressing accurate values by force of law, that law, namely, which prescribes what weight and fineness of metal is really a shilling, a pound, a franc, or a dollar. Of course the metal must also be specified, whether it be copper, silver, or gold, because equal weights of these several metals, though of the same fineness, have different values.

Now it is evident that since the monetary unit serves as the ultimate standard by which all values are to be measured; since it is also the concrete value which the law assumes to be specified whenever the name affixed to it is used, and since the use of that name dollar enters into every transaction, engagement, and contract relating to money, this unit must necessarily be accurately defined as to value, and must be permanently established.

* The ideal shilling, viz.: the one-twentieth of a pound sterling, is really the English unit. The shilling coins now in use are of silver and have only a token value.

DEFINITENESS AND STABILITY OF VALUE 85

Contracts to pay or to receive money at a future time would never be entered into if the actual value to be paid or received at that time cannot be relied upon by both parties. Such contracts are essential to the free and full play of the forces of industrial production and consumption, upon which trade and commerce depend, and upon which, also, the prosperity of the people depends. To introduce uncertainty, therefore, into men's minds as to the monetary unit, is to check all the springs of enterprise, to retard all the movements of trade, to hinder the free interchange of commodities, and in that way to obstruct and curtail both production and consumption, to the disorder of industry, and to the damage of the people in all ranks of life. The establishment of a monetary unit or fixed standard of value is, therefore, the highest duty of governments, and the more numerous and diverse the forms of money in use, the more imperative does this duty become. There is, however, another element required to make any particular kind of money really good, namely, invariability in its purchasing power, stability of value. This quality of money is not recognizable by a child, or by an uneducated person, because there is no mark, either on coins or paper money, by which the presence or absence of the quality is indicated. The test as to currency, *i.e.*, whether the particular form of money in question passes current, does not suffice for determining the presence of the quality of stability of value, since what passes current to-day may not do so to-morrow; and again, depreciated money often continues to pass current, though its value, *i.e.*, its purchasing power, is all the time becoming less and less.

We are so accustomed to measure values and to express all variations of value by money, that it requires a little effort to conceive of money itself as varying in value, but such a conception will be by no means difficult, if regard is had to the distinction between price and value which has been already pointed out. Price is the exponent of the computed relation between value in the commodity and value in money; it is not always, perhaps it is never, possible to ascertain absolutely what this relation is, but price expresses the estimate of it arrived at by the conflict of opinions among those who deal in the commodity, some being interested to extol its money value, and others equally interested to depreciate it.

Every relation implies at least two objects between which the relation subsists, it also implies something common to them both, to serve as a medium of comparison. The two objects in this case are money and some commodity, say a watch, and what they have in common is value. When we compare the value of any commodity with that of money, we express the result of the comparison in money value, that is, price. So we say, "This watch is worth $100," "The price is $100," yet we can conceive of a man who has $100 saying, "The price of this $100 is such and such a watch."

The jeweler buys $100 with his watch when the customer buys the watch with $100.

Variations of the relation expressed by price may, of course, be caused by a change in the value of the article, or by a change in the value of the money, or by changes in both values. This is a matter of the utmost importance, to be completely understood and remembered, because we are so accustomed to estimate values entirely by prices that even well-informed persons are misled into supposing that they are always interconvertible terms. In any event, price is never more than estimated value, and, too, value estimated by comparison with the value of the money in which the price is expressed.

Those who are old enough to remember the prices prevailing on either side of Mason and Dixon's line during the late war, should have no difficulty in discriminating between value and price. The value of a ten-dollar gold piece never varied between 1860 and 1865, but its price, whether in greenbacks or Confederate currency, varied often and greatly during that time. Not only did the price vary, but it was always varying and everywhere uncertain; facts that, being truly interpreted, mean that the two currencies in which these prices were expressed were themselves uncertain in value as well as variable in value.

This point being made clear, it is evident that good money should not only stand the test of passing current, but it should also be definite in value and possess the further quality of stability of value. The possession of this latter quality is essential to good money, because we measure all other values by money, and unless it is itself unchangeable in value, we cannot depend upon it as a measure of other value; we can never know whether the price asked for what we have to buy is correct or not, nor how much we ought to ask for what we have to sell in order to get full value.

Since stability of value is an essential property of good money, the question arises, how is this obtained? And then there is another question behind this, namely, how are the people to distinguish between money that possesses this quality and money that lacks it? Stability of value is assured, when, as has been the case in England for nearly half a century, only one metal is used for money, or when, as has been the case in the United States since January, 1879, all the different kinds of money in use are maintained constantly at a parity of value with the monetary unit.

The practical test of stability in the value of the money in use is general stability in prices. There is no other test, nor can any better be conceived. When prices of commodities generally, without distinction as to relative supply and demand, advance, the money is declining in value; when such prices decline, the money is advancing in value; when they fluctuate together, all up and then all down, the money is fluctuating in value.

DEFINITENESS AND STABILITY OF VALUE

When the Confederate currency was constantly declining in value, all prices advanced, *pari passu*, until there was nothing cheap enough to be bought with the entire issue. Before this final evaporation of all value, it had been said in Richmond that a man going to market needed a basket for his money, but might bring home dinner for the family in his purse. Many a family realized the truth underlying this too keenly to appreciate the humor of the illustration. Between 1862 and 1864 greenbacks also steadily declined in purchasing power, and after the latter date they were constantly variable in this respect, wherefore prices throughout the United States rose from 1862 to 1864, and afterward fluctuated with the gold premium.

CHAPTER IX.

THE MONETARY UNIT

Whenever the money of any community consists, as ours does, of elements diverse in material, form, and intrinsic value, such as coins of different metal and paper notes, these elements must be maintained in harmony among themselves, as respects their purchasing power or money force, in order that the people's money, as a whole, may possess and retain the essential qualities of definiteness and stability of value. It is manifest that if any two kinds of dollars, while continuing to circulate side by side, should come to differ in purchasing power, then the term dollar would lose its definiteness as an expression of value, and there would ensue throughout the community indescribable confusion and contention as to which of the two should be paid and received as the true dollar. There would be two measures for determining a dollar's worth of everything, whether it be of labor or of the ten thousand objects daily, and almost hourly, bought and sold in all parts of the land; and no one would be competent to decide between the two. It would be still worse if there were in circulation several kinds of dollars each having a different value.

It has, however, been ascertained, by the experience of past generations, that even two kinds of money cannot possibly continue circulating side by side when once they are recognized as differing in purchasing power, *i.e.*, in money force, because the moment any inequality of value among the ingredients of a mixed currency is discovered or even suspected to exist, that moment everybody hoards the more valuable and hurries to pass off the less valuable of those ingredients, so that in a short time the former are sifted out from the circulation and disappear, while only the least valuable ingredient of all remains accessible to the people, thus debasing the money of the community and correspondingly affecting all measurements of values, *i.e.*, raising the prices of everything.

This natural law was first pointed out by Sir Thomas Gresham, three hundred years ago, and by reference to history it is found to have asserted itself, both before his time and since, whenever and wherever two or more kinds of money, circulating together, have been perceived, or even suspected, to have lost, or to be likely to lose, their equipoise in value. So universal and inevitable is the operation of this law that people of all lands and all tongues have defied edicts, statutes, and even military force; they have put aside old prejudices and disregarded usage, tradition, patriotism, public spirit, even what appears to be their own immediate welfare and prosperity, in the irresistible impulse to pursue a course of individual conduct which, when practised by all, inevitably results in restricting the money circulating in the community to the least valuable and least desirable of its elements.*

* "The silver coin, which was then the standard coin of the realm, was in a state at which the boldest and most enlightened statesmen stood aghast.

"Till the reign of Charles the Second our coin had been struck by a process as old as the thirteenth century. The metal was divided with shears and afterward shaped and stamped by the hammer. In these operations much was left to the eye and hand of the workman. It necessarily happened that some pieces contained a little more and some a little less than the just quantity of silver: few pieces were exactly round; and the rims were not marked. It was therefore in the course of years discovered that to clip the coin was one of the easiest and most profitable kinds of fraud; and, about the time of the Restoration, people began to observe that a large proportion of the crowns, half-crowns and shillings which were passing from hand to hand had undergone some slight mutilation.

"That was a time fruitful of experiments and inventions in all the departments of science. A great improvement in the mode of shaping and striking the coin was suggested. A mill, which to a great extent superseded the human hand, was set up in the Tower of London. This mill was worked by horses, and would doubtless be considered by modern engineers as a rude and feeble machine. The pieces which it produced, however, were among the best in Europe. It was not easy to counterfeit them; and, as their shape was exactly circular, and their edges were inscribed with a legend, clipping was not to be apprehended. The hammered coins and the milled coins were current together. They were received without distinction in public, and consequently in private, payments. The financiers of that age seem to have expected that the new money, which was excellent,

In such cases, of course, the sifting and hoarding is done chiefly by those who are the first to perceive the tendency toward divergence in value, and as these are generally bankers and other dealers in money, they reap whatever benefit can possibly be got out of the sifting and the hoarding, while the refuse of the circulation is

would soon displace the old money, which was much impaired. Yet any man of plain understanding might have known that, where the State treats perfect coin and light coin as of equal value, the perfect coin will not drive the light coin out of circulation, but will itself be driven out. . . .

"The politicians of that age, however, generally overlooked these very obvious considerations. They marvelled exceedingly that everybody should be so perverse as to use light money in preference to good money. In other words, they marvelled that nobody chose to pay twelve ounces of silver when ten would serve the turn. The horse in the Tower still paced his rounds. Fresh wagon-loads of choice money still came forth from the mill; and still they vanished as fast as they appeared. Great masses were melted down; great masses exported; great masses hoarded: but scarcely one new piece was to be found in the till of a shop, or in the leathern bag which the farmer carried home after the cattle fair. . . . During many years this evil went on increasing. At first it was disregarded: but it at length became an insupportable curse to the country. It was to no purpose that the rigorous laws against coining and clipping were rigorously executed. At every session that was held at the Old Bailey terrible examples were made. . . . One morning seven men were hanged and one woman burned for clipping. But all was vain. . . .

"The evil proceeded with constantly accelerating velocity. At length in the autumn of 1695 it could hardly be said that the country possessed, for practical purposes, any measure of the value of commodities. It was a mere chance whether what was called a shilling was really tenpence, sixpence, or a groat."— *Macaulay's History of England*, chap. xxi.

put off upon laborers, artisans, farmers, and other plain folk. These classes, constituting the bulk of the population, must either make out with the refuse or go without money altogether, and they thus become forced to suffer inconvenience and loss by reason of that uncertainty and confusion as to all values which invariably attends the dissolution of a mixed currency. As every mixed currency is in danger, more or less, of having the equilibrium of value among its ingredients disturbed, at some time or other, by causes beyond the control of the government and people, and of thus suffering dissolution, such currencies have been, by many writers and statesmen, altogether condemned as mischievous to the people, and the only grounds upon which they have been justified are these four : First, the convenience to the people of having several kinds of money from which to select whichever best suits each occasion; secondly, economy in the use of one or both of the precious metals; thirdly, raising the volume of the circulation above what could be maintained by using only one of these metals; fourthly, the various considerations, whatever they may be, that support the doctrines of the bimetallists.

Without discussing here the positive or relative force properly due to either of these four postulates, it is evident that they all rest upon the assumption that such a mixed currency as they severally uphold is advantageous to the people.

THE MONETARY UNIT 95

If this is true, then the good of the people requires that whatever may be the ingredients of the currency their coequal value should be preserved, because, if this is disturbed, one or more of these ingredients will be eliminated, and this will defeat every object of a mixed currency. It follows, therefore, that all who for any reason favor our present mixed currency, must, by logical necessity, assent to the proposition that the good of the people requires that the elements composing it be preserved in harmony of value, since, because of Gresham's law, that is the sole condition upon which the integrity of the currency can be secured and the volume of the circulation maintained.

This point being established, it remains next to inquire how this desired object can be practically accomplished, and the answer is, only by the establishment and maintenance of a monetary unit, or a unit of value, corresponding with the denominational unit of the money system of the community.

A monetary unit is a definite weight of a particular metal of a certain fineness, established by law, to be the actual substantive value designated by the term which is the denominational unit of the money system of the country. The denominational unit of our money system is the term *dollar;* the monetary unit, or unit of value, is 25.8 grains of gold, nine-tenths fine. It may be interesting to trace the history of this matter in the laws of the United States. About the time the Revolutionary war broke out the public men and journalists of the different colonies had begun to call the inhabitants of these colonies distinctively *Americans,* and to speak of their common country as *America,* but these terms reflected no actual unity of origin, sentiment, or society among the people. They arose merely from an aspiration toward nationality that appears pathetic when contrasted with the actual condition of the communities which cherished it.

The thirteen colonies were not only under distinct governments, but they were isolated communities, each having a history and traditions of its own, some peculiarity of population, industry, and religion ; its own centre of influence, and its own group of public men, intent chiefly upon local usefulness and celebrity. Under these conditions the people of the colonies, until their quarrel with Great Britain, had little in common, save their experience with respect to money, and it is useful to recall this experience now, because it is the foundation of our monetary legislation, and also because it illustrates most vividly the cardinal principles which underlie this whole subject.

The money circulating in the colonies consisted of British, French, and Spanish coins, chiefly the latter, and also of paper bills of credit emitted by the different colonial governments. In all history there is nothing so instructive, in respect to money, as the account of the various currencies that from time to time vexed the souls of the people and thwarted all industrial efforts in these enterprising and resolute communities.* Experience, therefore, impressed the Fathers of the American Union with the importance of a new departure in financial management, and hence we find that the Articles of Confederation, which stand at the threshold of our national existence, vested in Congress " the sole and exclusive right and power of regulating the alloy and value of coin struck by their own authority or by that of the respective States." The States not being yet ready to surrender the prerogative of coinage (although unable to avail themselves of it) nevertheless recognized the necessity of co-ordinating their several coinages with each other, and with that of the Congress, and, as it were, fusing into one monetary whole the diverse elements composing what was then the only money of the people.†

A further and more effective step in the same direction was afterward made by providing in the Constitution that " the Congress shall have power to coin money, regulate the value thereof, and of foreign coins," and that " no State shall coin money, emit bills of credit, or make anything but

---

* See Money, p. 304 et seq. F. A. Walker, New York, 1878. Money: Its Laws and History, p. 429 et seq. H. V. Poore, New York, 1877. Sumner's American Currency.

† The Congress of the Confederation had, on July 6, 1785, established the dollar as the ideal money unit, and on August 8, 1786, an act was passed to create a coinage, but nothing practical was done under it.

gold and silver coin a tender in payment of debts." Even up to 1789 no gold and silver had been mined in the United States, and the metallic money in circulation consisted almost wholly of foreign coins, chiefly Spanish dollars, which passed at slightly different rates in different parts of the country under various Colonial and State laws, so that the first of the above-quoted clauses of the Constitution is a distinct recognition of the obligation naturally resting upon the government, to unify and consolidate the currency, which was even more diverse in form, though less so in the intrinsic value of its several ingredients, than that with which we have to deal in 1893; while the second was evidently intended to erect a barrier against the introduction into the general mass of the people's money of any element which could not be always so regulated in value as to be maintained at a level with all the other elements.

In pursuance of these wise provisions of the Constitution, Congress, by the Act of April 2d, 1792, established the dollar as the "unit of the money of account" for the whole United States, and from that day to this all our conceptions of the value of things, all our computations and contracts, have been expressed in dollars. From 1792 to 1862 legal provision was made from time to time for preserving uniformity in the conventional value of whatever different kinds of money enjoyed the recognition of the Federal government; but during that interval there arose many banks chartered by the separate States, and the notes issued by these banks, though not sanctioned by any Federal law, constituted a very large part of the currency circulating among the people. Though expressed in dollars and redeemable in United States coin, those bank-notes were by no means of uniform money force everywhere, nor were they always constant in such force at the same place, which caused great inconvenience and loss to the people, especially to farmers, laborers, tradesmen, and artisans, who were constrained by force of circumstances to accept this sort of money in payment for their products, their services, and their wares.*

After 1862 monetary affairs became greatly disordered by the war, coin disappeared from general circulation, while United States Treasury notes on one side, and Confederate States Treasury notes on the other, became, under the operation of Gresham's law, the only kind of money available to the people at large, notwithstanding that, according to the best estimate, the gold coin in the country was never less than $200,000,000.† When the war ended, in 1865, the Confederate currency was worthless, and the greenbacks were so depreciated that $100 in that currency would buy only about $70 in

* See Report Ways and Means Committee, H. R., 1831, on President's Message relating to rechartering of the Bank of the United States. Also, Money: Its Laws and History, p. 527 et seq., and p. 544 et seq. H. V. Poore, New York, 1877.

† See Report of the Secretary of the Treasury, 1886, p. 79.

gold coin of the United States. The National Bank notes, being redeemable in greenbacks, conformed in conventional value to that depreciated currency.*

The people of the re-United States consequently found themselves compelled to buy at a premium of about forty per cent. whatever amount they needed of money conformed in value to the dollar which the Act of 1792 had established as the unit of account, and a great many of them needed such money, either to carry on foreign trade, to pay the duty on imports, which the government exacted in gold, or to travel beyond the limits of the United States. The depreciation of the only currency obtainable by the people at large in payment for their products and services lifted up all prices above the plane of real commercial value in such a way as to place industrial producers in this country at a great disadvantage with those abroad. It also placed all the people, in their capacity of buyers of what they consumed, at similar but still greater disadvantage, in comparison with their condition before 1861 and since 1879. The chief weight of this disadvantage rested upon the poorer classes in the towns, and upon farmers, artisans, and the like.

It was because of the losses and inconveniences resulting from this condition of things that the people, with cheerful unanimity, undertook, and

* Every redeemable currency conforms in value to the value of the medium of its redemption.

carried through, the painful process of specie resumption, which is only another name for the restoration of the dollar as "the unit of the money of account" to the value it had in 1792, as preserved by the successive changes made by the Acts of June 28, 1834, January 18, 1837, February 21, 1853, and February 12, 1873, in the weight and fineness of the metals selected for expressing this value. Whoever supposes that the people of this country are unable to see and to appreciate the consequences of monetary legislation may well ponder this recent episode in our history and take note that the permanent respect and confidence of the American masses is obtained only by statesmen who counsel wisely in matters affecting our general industrial and financial interests, and that politicians who pander to such local and ephemeral aberrations as the greenback fanaticism and the silver craze surely sink into disrepute and obscurity.

The Resumption Act, and the measures taken in pursuance of it, restored to the people substantially the money intended to be guaranteed to them by the Constitution, and the last of the series of acts fixing the value of this money, based it on a monetary unit, viz., 25.8 grains of gold, nine-tenths fine. This has remained until to-day the monetary unit of the United States, and by this all values have been measured and computed since January 1, 1879.

The importance to the people of selecting and

adhering to a certain weight and fineness of one metal as the monetary unit, arises wholly out of the fact that their money is manifold in form, substance, and intrinsic value. If we had only gold coins, or only silver coins; if these were of uniform fineness, and proportioned to each other in weight, according to the denominations of the monetary scale or system, and if all the paper money was securely redeemable in whichever of these two coinages constituted the sole legal tender, the unit of that coinage would be the monetary unit of the country. Our four kinds of money, however, differ in intrinsic value, and therefore they can be maintained at uniform conventional and legal value only by investing one of the two metallic coinages (gold and silver) with the character of a basis or standard of value, and by force of law conferring upon the other elements of the currency values representative of the actual value intrinsically present in that selected to be the standard.

The government is by no means free to select either of the two coinages as the standard, but must select that of greater intrinsic value, or else, under Gresham's law, those coins will disappear from circulation. If instead of 25.8 grains of gold 412½ grains of silver had been made the monetary unit in 1873, we should now have no gold coin at all in circulation,* because, while legislative force and the credit of the government may supplement

* There are no gold coins circulating in Mexico or India.

intrinsic value they cannot be applied in abatement of it; hence by operation of natural law, overriding all political and other considerations, every community must take its monetary unit from that element in the currency which is intrinsically the most valuable. The monetary unit once established becomes the standard for measuring all values expressed in money, and thus it enters into all business and financial transactions, arrangements, and contracts; hence it should be always preserved at substantially the same level of value.

We have seen that definiteness and stability of value are essential qualities of money, and since all money existing in the form of a mixed currency conforms in value to the monetary unit, this unit must of course possess these qualities in the highest degree. The haste of modern life, the velocity attained by the currents of business, produce a tendency to definiteness in quantities, in values, and even in terms, which is as characteristic of the age as it is a necessary condition of order and confidence amidst the throng of transactions that must be rushed through the straitened hours of every day.

The progress toward simplification and method, which begun when coins were substituted for scales and weights in the measurement of copper, silver, and gold, has been continued constantly in the direction of improving the coins, perfecting their accuracy, and fortifying their permanency in respect to value, and its logical conclusion is now reached in the adoption of a monetary unit, by means of which several kinds of money, varying in intrinsic value, are co-ordinated as to legal value, and their solidarity in the currency is established and preserved.

It may be well, just here, to point out that as there can be but one unit in each monetary system, there should be but one monetary unit in each country. If any doubt this, let them imagine two such units; then either these must be of identical value, or of different values; if they are of identical value, they are mere duplicates, equivalent to, and reducible to a single unit; hence one or the other of the two is superfluous. But if the two monetary units differ in value, then we have two meanings to one word, and to that word, which of all words of similar import, has been presumably selected by the law to be confined to one definite and invariable meaning. Beyond this; if you have two monetary units of different values, then you have two monetary systems, each with a unit of its own, and the people who have to use these two systems will be subjected to the inconvenience of having to translate values expressed according to one system into the equivalent expressions of the other system.

It would be like the pleadings in the old courts at New Orleans, when half the jury understood only English, and the other half understood only French, so that evidence and argument had to be addressed to one half, and translated for the benefit of the other half; a system which maintained a large body of professional interpreters, but was very costly to litigants. In the same way, a people subjected to a dual monetary unit would have to maintain an army of money-changers out of the earnings of legitimate industry. We had an example of this between 1862 and 1879, when we had in this country a dual monetary unit, one for the people generally, and another for the transactions connected with foreign commerce, including the payment of duties on imports. The Gold Exchange, and all the horde of speculators and exchange and bullion dealers who made and lost fortunes during those years, were the product of this dual monetary unit, and the cost of it all to the legitimate industry of the country is beyond computation.

The duty of the government, therefore, in respect to this matter, is to establish a monetary unit, and to provide against its being changed except by such universal consent as is requisite to effect a constitutional amendment. In selecting the unit many considerations arise which can be better considered after the important subject of value has been fully inquired into; but meanwhile it is well to glance at the scope of this question.

Since all the various forms of our money are used for measuring values, the dollar bears to values the relation which an inch bears to measurements of extension. Now, from an industrial point of view, we may regard the United States as a great workshop, and its people generally as workmen, each of whom must constantly fit and shape his work, as to value, with a view to the value of some work being simultaneously executed by other workmen; and money is the value-rule by which alone these indispensable adjustments may be accurately and certainly made. Now imagine an ordinary workshop where the foot-rules are not on the same scale; where the unit of linear measure — the inch — is not definite nor fixed, so that the inches and the feet marked on one man's rule do not correspond with the inches and the feet marked on the rule of another man engaged on a different part of the same work. Would there not be inextricable confusion and wrangling among the men, attended with spoiling of material and consequent loss and vexation to the proprietor? Would there not be necessarily a spontaneous halt in the work, and a simultaneous demand that some one of the various inches be selected as a standard, and that all rules that differed from the standard be banished, and even destroyed utterly?

Now money, as a measure of value, sustains toward the specialized and differentiated industries of this country, relations precisely like those which foot-rules sustain to the specialized and differentiated employments into which the work of a great machine-shop is distributed, and, therefore, if the dollar, which is "the unit of the money of account," lacks definiteness and stability of value, the currency will be incessantly distributing over the country inaccurate value-rules. An industrial people, subjected by their government to the use of such a currency, are just as badly treated as would be the hands in a machine-shop who should be furnished with defective and inaccurate foot-rules, and then held accountable for material spoiled and time lost by misfits.

One step further: while the United States may be regarded as a great workshop, yet it is only a branch of the still greater workshop of the world at large. The extent to which our industries are correlated with those of other countries may be seen from the magnitude of our foreign commerce. The products of our industry which are exported, and the imported products of the industry of other countries, are interchanged commodities. This interchange depends upon comparison of values, like that obtaining in domestic trade, and, as we have seen, comparison of values is rendered possible only by the use of a common monetary unit.

Our agricultural, mining, manufacturing, and other industries, are more or less concerned in our foreign commerce, hence the people engaged in these industries are to that extent fellow-workmen with consumers and producers in other nations. The value-rule in use among us should, therefore, bear a definite, known, and unchangeable relation to the value-rules in use among the people with whom we trade. While it would be more convenient to have but one monetary unit for all the world, it is not necessary to do so. Different nations may still retain those they are accustomed to, but it is absolutely essential that each of these should be immutable in real value, and that they should all be alike in material, for identity of metal can alone insure identity of intrinsic value in equal weights. The pound sterling, the franc, the mark, and the dollar need not agree in value, but they should be only degrees in one common and fixed value-scale, so that it can never be a matter of doubt or uncertainty what is the equivalent of a pound in dollars, marks, or francs, nor what fraction of a dollar is the precise equivalent of a franc, a mark, or a shilling. How this may be secured will more fully appear hereafter.

CHAPTER X.

LEGAL TENDER

The term "legal tender" is a technical expression signifying that which the law prescribes to be paid or tendered in order to discharge a debt, satisfy a judgment, fulfil a money contract, or pay taxes. A system of law that recognizes the obligation of contracts is incomplete unless it also enforces their performance. When the contract is to pay a sum of money, the law requires the stipulated sum of money to be paid specifically. When the contract is to do a certain thing, the law requires that thing to be done specifically, and when it is impossible to enforce specific performance modern laws require the defaulter to pay a money indemnity. Every person under contract to pay money, or, under judgment, to pay a sum of money or a money indemnity, in default of specific performance of contract, is a debtor for the money thus to be paid, and the law which adjudges him a debtor must settle what is to constitute full and sufficient payment whereby he may be relieved from the obligation of debt.

Hence it comes that in all countries where the laws recognize the obligation of contracts, and enforce performance of them, the laws also prescribe a legal tender money, and it is obvious that the main principle underlying the establishment of a legal tender is that it is something fixed, something upon the steadfastness of which people may depend when coming under an obligation or a liability. Fixed as to what? Steadfast as to what? Necessarily as to value, because value is the only quality pertinent to the effectiveness of a legal tender. Our commonest money obligations, promissory notes, drafts, bills of exchange, contain the acknowledgment of the signer that he has received value for them; "value received" is an invariable phrase in every such instrument. Every bond, every contract, rests upon an acknowledgment of value received, in consideration whereof the contract is undertaken or the bond executed.

The very object, therefore, of a legal tender law —what the French call its *raison d'être* (reason for existing); what the old school-men would have called its "final cause" (cause for which it was enacted)—must necessarily be to establish a fixed and immutable measure, or standard, by which the value repaid or returned may be compared with and made equal to the value acknowledged to have been received, and in other cases by which the value paid in satisfaction of a debt, or a judgment, may be compared and equalized with the value agreed or adjudged to be payable therefor.

This being the nature and the object of all legal tender laws, reason itself requires that when such a law gives legal tender force to several kinds of money, these kinds of money must be always preserved at equal value, for if they are not so preserved the nature of the legal tender law is violated and its essential object is defeated. This is not only a requirement of reason, but it is also demanded by that spirit of justice which is the soul of law and should be the animating principle of all legislation. Legal tender laws control the execution of contracts, and every contract embraces two or more persons, sustaining to each other complementary relations, between or among whom justice requires that these relations be kept in equilibrium. Every debt, every indemnity, payable in money, necessarily involves, on one side, one or more persons bound to pay, and, on the opposite side, one or more persons entitled to receive; for every obligation there is a right, every dollar to be paid is also a dollar to be received.

The essence of these reciprocal relations is equality, and that equality which is mutually acknowledged to have existed at the initial stage of the contract, namely, equality of the value received at the date of the note or bond, with the value agreed to be returned at its maturity, lives through the life of the instrument which represents the contract, so that, when the period of its temporary alienation has expired, the value transferred may return unimpaired whence it came. The whole theory of a money penalty for default of specific performance rests upon the doctrine here set forth, and this doctrine also underlies all taxation, for without fixed value in the medium of payment the taxing power can neither provide adequately for the public needs nor gauge the burden laid on the tax-payers.

At every stage of this inquiry we have found one and the same truth underlying the surface wherever we have probed, and that is, that money is sought only for its power to command its worth in something else. Not money but money's worth, not the dollar but the dollar's worth, is the motor of industry, the propelling force behind human enterprise and endeavor. This truth is the key to the obligations of governments in respect to legal tender money; they are bound to preserve its value, its true worth. The name of the coin, the denomination of the note, is absolutely naught; the value is the essence of the matter; equality of value, not identity of substance, between the thing borrowed and the thing returned; equality of value, not specific identity, between the thing promised and the thing performed, will alone content the avidity of justice for what is right.

A practical question arises here: Under our laws four kinds of money are made legal tender—gold coins, silver standard dollar coins, coin certificates, and greenbacks. The doctrine just laid down obligates the government to preserve an equality of value among these, but, at present, the intrinsic values of the gold and silver coins are wide apart, while the coin certificates, and, according to some authorities, the greenbacks also, are redeemable in either gold or silver dollars, at the option of the government. Now it is possible, and by many considered probable, that, under the continued purchase of silver bullion, following the compulsory coinage of standard silver dollars, it will become, sooner or later, impracticable to preserve an equality of value between the gold and silver coins, unless new means are adopted to that end. Gold may become demonetized and revert to the condition of a commodity, in which case the government, not being able to take in enough gold in its revenues to redeem the greenbacks in that coinage, may have to redeem them in standard silver dollars.

In this case the equality of value of the four kinds of money will be dissolved, while, as has been shown, the government is under the highest obligation, both of reason and of justice, to maintain the four at the same value, in order that they may all be available equally, as the law promised, to serve as legal tender for obligations incurred when they were of the same value. It is, of course, obvious that in such an event the government could never pay the premium on whatever gold might be required to liquidate all such contracts, nor is there any other way in which the loss to the people can be made up, if once the equilibrium of value among the four kinds of money should be destroyed; hence, now, while the equilibrium exists, Congress is bound to use every means to preserve it, and the people should exact legislation to this end while yet there is time to prevent so irremediable a disaster.

However unstable the equilibrium between the gold and silver coinage may have become under the disturbing influences exerted by financial changes abroad and short-sighted legislation at home, it is still in the power of the government to restore its stability.

1st. Let all compulsory coinage laws and silver purchase laws be repealed. This will relieve the Treasury of the strain upon it made by these laws, and in that way fortify the credit of the executive branch of the government. It will also relieve apprehension as to our getting down to the standard silver-dollar basis, which will fortify the credit of the legislative branch of the government by furnishing evidence of its intelligence and its regard for justice.

2d. Let these two branches of the government unite in such legislation as will make twenty-five and eight-tenths grains of gold, nine hundred fine, the permanently settled monetary unit of this country, and in affirming that the government has guaranteed, and is bound to maintain, the standard silver dollars at a parity in legal tender quality with this standard gold dollar, by maintaining their interconvertibility at the Treasury. If these things are done, the credit of the government thus reinforced will be sufficient to support so much of the nominal value of the standard silver dollars as now overhangs their intrinsic value, and the solidarity of our coinage will be strengthened and perpetuated.

3d. The good work accomplished by these measures would be perfected, and the people's money would for all time be secured against legislative attack, if the Supreme Court should reverse its legal tender decision and limit Congress, as the States are limited, to gold and silver as legal tender money.

CHAPTER XI.

THE MATERIAL AND FORM OF MONEY

Since the government is charged with the duty of determining what the people's money shall be, it is well to inquire at this point what latitude of choice exists as to material and form. Disregarding for the moment the numerous substances tried and abandoned during the world's gropings after a suitable material for money, we may assume that at the present day no enlightened government would attempt to use anything as money except coins of gold, silver, and copper (or nickel), or else paper suitably prepared and printed to protect the public against counterfeits. It may be said, therefore, that the material of money nowadays must be either metal or paper.

There is not much more latitude of choice as to form; metal used as money is cut and stamped into coins, of which the weight and fineness are definitely established by law; paper used as money is especially manufactured, printed from engraved plates, and attested as genuine by the signatures of officials commissioned for the purpose. Narrow as those limits appear to be, there is yet room within them for the introduction of elements of mischief, wide-spread in their effects and disastrous to industry, as well as to social welfare. The history of all ages is full of instances in which the rapacity of rulers brought distress upon their people through the debasement of metallic coinages, while the evil consequences of issues of paper money are among the saddest episodes in the annals of modern nations. It is important, therefore, to inquire what principles should govern the coinage of metals and the creation of paper currency.

Before proceeding to these inquiries, however, it is necessary to point out the difference between these two kinds of money: Coins possess intrinsic value; that is, the substance of which they are made is valuable in itself. Whether coined or not, gold, silver, and copper are valuable as metals, and their value is nearly the same all the world over. Paper money has practically no intrinsic value; its money-force depends upon law, or upon the financial credit of the government, or the credit of a bank; sometimes certificates, representing coins of gold or silver deposited in the Treasury, and redeemable in such coins, are used as money. Paper money generally expresses an obligation or a promise; it usually implies a contract or a trust, and its value, derived wholly from these, depends for its continuance upon the public confidence that the promise or obligation will be fulfilled, the trust or contract executed. Beyond the limits within which this confidence suffices to give it currency, paper money, whether in the form of Bank of England notes, greenbacks, National Bank notes, or coin certificates, loses its money function; it has no force to pay wages, or to pass from hand to hand in the ordinary course of daily traffic.

There is another very important difference between coins and paper money. The value of coins, being in their substance, is not affected by or dependent on what is stamped or imprinted upon them, for the devices on a coin constitute merely a label as to fineness and weight, put there in order to save the time and expense of testing the weight and fineness of each coin every time it passes from one person to another; but the value of paper money is altogether determined by what is printed on it; change this and the value is changed accordingly; remove it, and all value vanishes from the defaced paper. But paper money may have its value reduced or destroyed without change of purport, for what is printed on the paper is an obligation, or promise, or contract to pay money, and if the promisor, whether a government or a bank, cannot or will not pay, or quibbles about the medium of payment, or if, through design or ignorance, the laws relating to the matter are tampered with, the value of the engagement will be correspondingly affected; while, on the other hand, the intrinsic value of coins can be neither changed nor destroyed by the acts or omissions of governments, banks, or individuals. Coined metal is beyond the reach of political strife; it is free from danger by reason of disaster, panic, or war. Earthquakes, revolutions, the rise and fall of empires, have been powerless to impair by a fraction the value inhering in the coins sewed in the garments of trembling towns-people or hidden in the huts of a terrified peasantry. Here is the peculiar merit of metallic money; its value is independent of the will and the fate of princes, of governments, and of corporations.

Paper currency, on the other hand, is created by statute; every note has value conferred upon it solely by the stroke of the pen recording an official signature. A greenback or bank-note of $1,000 contains no more paper and ink than one for only $5; it costs no more to produce the one than the other; the difference of intrinsic value is either nil or inappreciable. Paper money, however widely disseminated among the people, forever draws its force and virtue from a source absolutely controlled by the government, just as the lights of a great city depend upon a continuous supply of gas or electricity from some central station. The money life of such currency depends wholly upon the continuous sustaining force of the law; interrupt this, and it droops depreciated; cut off this support by repealing the law or disabling the government, and the currency dies, as the lights go out when the gas is turned off.

Every note that draws vitality from the law perishes with the repeal of the law, or with the downfall or bankruptcy of the government, even though it be locked in a hidden recess a thousand miles away from the seat of legislation or the theatre of revolution, and hence it is essential for the people that the government upon which paper money depends for maintenance of value should be trustworthy and stable.

In countries where the government is distinct from the people, where a few classes dominate and the masses are held in subjection, it is very difficult for the government to maintain paper money at its full value, or even at equable value. The people know, by the experience of previous generations, that no money is safe for them but that which carries its face value within itself. They are rightly afraid to trust a currency that may have its value turned off at Vienna or St. Petersburg while they are ploughing the land in some far Hungarian field, or tending cattle on the slopes of the Caucasus. The stability of the government may not be doubted, but the people do not trust their rulers. In our country the government is controlled by the people, and, therefore, the people do not distrust it in matters upon which there is an intelligent concurrence of public sentiment; but, unfortunately, financial principles are but little understood by the people and even by many of their representatives, and, as in private life, men suffer in fortune, and even in repu-

THE MATERIAL AND FORM OF MONEY 121

tation, by their own ignorance and mistakes, as well as by the ignorance and mistakes of their agents, so the people of the United States may have the miseries of a depreciated currency turned loose among them by a popular clamor for unwise legislation or by mere blunders at Washington.

A depreciated currency, whether metallic or paper, is the sum of all monetary evils; it is worse in its effects than war or pestilence; it seeks out and ruins the most secure and the most secluded; it brings widows and orphans to penury; it corrupts the virtuous, disheartens the industrious, destroys the helpless; it breeds rapacity, pampers vice, and sets up gambling as a substitute for profitable toil.

It may be asked, How may a government secure its people against the danger of the currency becoming depreciated? The answer is: A government should never make anything lawful money but coins of metal, and paper convertible into such coins on demand of the holder. Government may properly provide for the safe-keeping of coins deposited in its treasury, or in banks, and for supplying certificates of such deposits, so as to afford its people the convenience of transmitting large values in small compass, but it should never force upon them by law the use of a credit currency, unless under the stress of an overruling necessity, and then the ultimate convertibility into coin of such currency should be assured and studiously maintained. The reason for these conclusions will appear all through this treatise.

There is no reason, moreover, from a financial point of view, though there may be political reasons against it, why the United States government, after establishing, under constitutional sanction, an unchangeable monetary unit, should not provide in its laws for a system of banks of issue, which may supply to the currency an element adjustable in volume, under natural laws, to the varying needs of industry. This question will be subsequently discussed; but meanwhile, as a guide to the principles that should be observed in determining what the material and form of money should be, and with a view to exposing the baselessness of certain prejudices and popular errors, it may be well to review, briefly, the history of metallic money.

When Ephron named four hundred shekels of silver as the price of his land, he designated a weight of metal, not a number of coins. It was a great advance toward convenience when, about eleven hundred years after Abraham's time, money was first coined in pieces of definite weight, for then the scales of the money-changer could be dispensed with, and payments could be made by counting the coins instead of by weighing bars and lumps of metal; nevertheless, so little need was there apparently for the use of coins that the new invention spread but slowly from Argos, where it is said to have had its origin. The earliest coins appear to have been made of brass, and afterward of iron and copper; silver, being used only in large payments and passing by weight, was not coined until long afterward. The occasions for the use of silver as money were so infrequent in these early ages that no popular need would have been subserved by coining it, and for the same reason it was later still that gold coins came into use.

While the use of coins was tardily resorted to, and has been but slowly developed, the metals gold and silver were used in the arts and for personal ornament throughout Europe, Asia, and Africa in the remotest antiquity of which any trace has come down to us. They were so used also by the aboriginal races of North and South America, but nowhere in either of these two continents had they been coined into money up to less than four hundred years ago, when Europeans discovered the New World. It appears, therefore, that everywhere other uses of gold and silver preceded their use as money. Of course, as long as the principal demand for these metals was for fabrication into vessels and ornaments, dealers in them kept their stock in bars, ingots, or other masses, which wealthy men, like Abraham, acquired in trade for their sheep and cattle. It would have been bad economy to have incurred the expense of coinage, even if coinage had then been thought of, when in all probability the coins would very soon have been melted down and cast into vessels, or hammered out and cut into rings, armlets, and other trinkets, simply because these things were much more generally wanted than coins were.

In primitive times money had no general sphere of circulation, for nearly all labor was performed by slaves or dependants, so that no money was required for wages; personal service was requited, not by salaries paid in money, but by protection, shelter, and maintenance; but few industries were pursued for gain, and trade consisted largely of barter. Afterward, as industrial pursuits became varied, money came into use, as has heretofore been described (see Chapter V.), and at each stage the material of money bore a relation to the value of labor. Now industry has become almost universal and is infinitely varied, and each worker is entirely master of his own earnings, so that money is indispensable to the daily life of hundreds of millions of men, women, and children, and the material of money has increased in value with the rising value of the labor which it measures, and the increasing volume of the transactions it liquidates. The world has outgrown brass, iron, and copper, successively used as money, and these metals are now all too low in value, in proportion to their weight and bulk, to serve the needs of industry among the more advanced nations, although copper coins are still found in circulation among peoples less advanced. Gold and silver are the metals now chiefly used as money in Europe and America, and coins made of either metal are generally slightly more valuable than an equal weight of the same metal uncoined; hence coins are now seldom melted down or hammered and cut into ornaments, unless some vicious or ignorant coinage law contravenes the natural laws which determine the relative value of these two metals.*

The intrinsic value of gold and silver is not a mysterious quality conferred upon these metals providentially under the divine economy, with a view to confining mankind to the use of either or both of them as money; they are not as useful in other respects, nor as necessary to civilization and to human happiness as iron is. Iron possesses intrinsic value just as definite and just as firmly established as the intrinsic value of gold and silver, and iron was just as useful for money in Sparta as silver was in Athens. The common sense of the matter is, that mankind has become satisfied by experiment that silver and gold are the best metals to be used as money at the present time, and when, if ever, they become satisfied that either of them can be advantageously dispensed with for such use, that metal will cease to be used for money, and no

---

* In such a case the mint becomes merely a public and gratuitous assayer for dealers in bullion, both in the country that owns the mint and out of it.

amount of sentiment, no force of declamation, can prevent its disuse.

In international trade gold and silver bullion are almost as available as coins; indeed, unless the coins of one country are by law made current in another, coins outside of the country of their issue are rated entirely by their bullion value, which is determined by their fineness and weight, irrespective of the monetary denomination stamped upon them. In the United States English sovereigns or French twenty-franc pieces are valued as so much uncoined gold; in Europe American eagles are valued in like manner.

Our gold coins are worth as much abroad as at home, because here we rate them at their true bullion value in the world's market as is done abroad, but it is otherwise with our silver coins, which we rate above their bullion value. Here five silver dollars, ten half-dollars, or fifty dimes will buy as much as a five-dollar gold piece; but in Europe, at the present time, the quantity of silver required to buy what could be bought with a half-eagle, would make, in our coins, more than seven dollars and a half. Hence it is apparent that our silver coinage is not available in foreign trade, since the coins are worth more at home than abroad, and more than the bullion out of which they are made. A man who desires to place $1,-000 in London or Paris may do so by shipping there fifty (50) double-eagles, or one hundred (100) eagles, or two hundred (200) half-eagles, but if he had to ship standard silver dollars to the same value it would require more than 1,500 of them.

Of course, therefore, he will ship the gold rather than the silver, because while these several quantities of coins would be of equal value abroad, namely, $1,000, their value here is, for the gold pieces, $1,000; for the standard dollars, $1,250; and for half-dollars and dimes, $1,867.50. It follows that all silver coined in the United States becomes unavailable for export, and later on we shall perceive the importance of keeping in circulation among ourselves as much as we can afford of every sort of money that is available in the foreign trade.

It is only in modern times that paper money has come into use. A sketch of its history will be found in Chapter XIII.; but it may be well at this point to suggest some views as to paper money generally. All paper currency, whether issued by the government or by a bank, consists of due bills only; these due bills may be simply the government outlay, or they may represent taxes to be collected, or gold or silver coins deposited in the Treasury; or they may represent value in some other form received by the government or by the banks. History teaches that it is never entirely safe for any people to entrust the keeping of all their gold and silver to treasuries and banks, while they have nothing to show for it but a paper receipt; and it is always exceedingly unsafe for the people, especially farmers, artisans, and laboring men, who are not in the way of keeping up with financial changes, to become wholly dependent upon a currency that has neither gold nor silver behind it, but which consists wholly of paper representing future taxation, or which is based solely upon the credit of a government, or of a corporation under governmental control.

Some unthinking people are deceived by the talk of politicians who harp upon such phrases as "Any money is better than no money" and that "If money is made plentiful it will be easier to get." Only a moment's reflection should be needed to detect the fallacies in this silly talk. Every man, every child knows that money does not come into people's hands for nothing. To get money one must earn it by his labor or his brain, or else he must give something of value in exchange for it. If one man trades horses with another each is very careful to examine the animal that he is to receive, and he exerts all his powers not to be deceived into accepting one that is unsound or otherwise not equal in value to that which he parts with.

Now why should such a man forbear to exercise as to the money that he gets for his labor, his talents, or his property, the same degree of scrutiny with which he examines the horse he is trading for? Does a man put up with a bad horse in exchange for a good one simply because bad horses are plentiful? Are not bad horses harder to trade

THE MATERIAL AND FORM OF MONEY 129

away when they are plentiful than when they are scarce? Is a man's labor, or his crop, not always good value, and should they not at all times be paid for in money that has equally good value? Can a man afford to be indifferent as to whether the money he gets is always equally good? It is certain that bad money can never be so plentiful that wages paid in it will go as far when they are to be spent as wages paid in good money.

If the government supplies the money it ought to take care that all of it is equally good, and equally good at all times; but this cannot be depended upon unless the people understand the difference between good money and bad, and require their representatives to possess that knowledge also, and to apply it in legislation, where alone such knowledge can be applied effectively. It is essential that popular intelligence should direct legislation, and not remain inert until mischievous measures have already been adopted; for, as was shown in a previous chapter, a free people are no better off than the subjects of an autocrat when once their money is in circulation and begins to depreciate in consequence of its losing public confidence.

CHAPTER XII.

COINED MONEY

In the preceding chapter it has been shown that gold and silver are now practically established as the prime money metals of the world; that the requirements of industry at home, and of foreign commerce, compel our government to the use of these metals in its coinage; and we now proceed to consider how this is at present provided for, and what changes, if any, should be made in our laws in order to adapt them more perfectly to the needs of the people. The Act of February 12, 1873, supplemented by that of February 28, 1878, constitutes the present coinage laws of the United States. The former Act made the gold dollar of $25\frac{8}{10}$ grains, 900 * fine, the "unit of value," and fixed the weights of all coins now existing, except the "standard silver dollar," which owes its existence to the Act of February 28, 1878.

An understanding of the coinage law, sufficient for our immediate purpose, may be obtained by

* In all our coins, both gold and silver, there are 900 parts of pure metal and 100 parts alloy.

an inspection of the following table, showing the coins now established as legal tenders in the United States, the standard weight of each, and the value of each, as measured by the unit of value, viz., the gold dollar of $25\frac{8}{10}$ grains, 900 fine:

Metals, 900 Fine.	Denominations.	Standard Weights, Grains.	Value Measured by Unit of Value.	
			Legal Value.	Intrinsic Value.
Silver........	Dime,	38.58	$ .10	$ .06$\frac{2a}{}$
Silver........	Quarter-dollar,	96.45	.25	.15$\frac{2a}{}$
Silver........	Half-dollar,	192.90	.50	.30$\frac{4a}{}$
Silver........	Standard dollar,	412.50	1.00	.65
Gold.........	Dollar,	25.80	1.00	1.00
Gold.........	Quarter-eagle,	64.50	2.50	2.50
Gold.........	Half eagle,	129.	5.00	5.00
Gold.........	Eagle,	258.	10.00	10.00
Gold.........	Double-eagle,	516.	20.00	20.00

It appears from the foregoing table that while the legal value of the different coins conforms to their respective designations, their intrinsic value differs greatly. Legally, ten standard dollars of silver are equal to an eagle; intrinsically, an eagle is worth more than fifteen such dollars. Legally, a hundred dimes are as good as an eagle; intrinsically, the eagle exceeds in value one hundred and sixty-four dimes.

The question naturally presents itself, why is there such inequality of intrinsic value among coins constituting a single system of coinage, in which, of course, all parts should be consistent with each other. The answer is, in the first place, that the dimes, quarter-dollars, and half-dollars are subsidiary coins, legal tender for only small amounts, and these were intended originally to be of slightly less proportionate value than the gold dollar, because when that ratio was fixed silver was advancing in value, and if these pieces had been heavier they would have disappeared from circulation. In the second place, speaking broadly, it may be said that nearly the whole inequality has arisen since 1873, and is the consequence of a great decline in silver without corresponding changes in the coinage laws. The Act of 1878 affected only the dollar coin, and since that time silver has fallen about thirty per cent. when valued in gold.

It is needless here to enter upon the vexed question as to whether gold has advanced in value or silver has declined; all that concerns us at this stage of the inquiry is the fact that whereas, some years ago, $25\frac{8}{10}$ grains of gold was constantly being exchanged for $412\frac{1}{2}$ grains of silver, now $25\frac{8}{10}$ grains of gold will command in exchange more than $634\frac{1}{2}$ grains of silver. This fact concerns us deeply, because our laws use the term dollar to signify the value of $25\frac{8}{10}$ grains of gold, and the same term dollar to signify the value of $412\frac{1}{2}$ grains of silver. According to law, these quantities of the two metals, respectively, are of equal value, when, according to fact, the ratio of their value is as 100 to 65.

The effect of this state of things is that the term dollar is in danger of losing that definiteness and precision as an expression of value which it should possess and permanently retain unvaried, in order that it may serve the purpose intended by its designation in the Act of April 2, 1792, as the "unit of the money of account." That act is the very foundation, and the only foundation, of all the dealings of the people with respect to money and other values, from that day to this. The term dollar has become assimilated with the living organism of American industry; it is incorporated into our daily speech, our habits of business, of thought, and of action; our methods of computation, and our system of reckoning. It has been recognized and conformed to in all legislation for nearly a hundred years, and to-day the adults, and many children, in our whole population of 70,000,000, are daily and hourly depending, in matters of momentous importance to them, upon the fixed idea of value associated with this word *dollar;* hence there is no computing the confusion and distress that will ensue upon its losing the essential qualities, *definiteness* and *precision* as to value.

To understand the present position, and the necessity for remedial legislation, it is only necessary to consider that intrinsic value alone constitutes natural, and therefore, permanent money force, and hence that our different coins may come to be rated by the bullion value of the metal contained in each. This rating would make a standard silver dollar equal to $16\frac{67}{100}$ grains of gold, while, as has been said, it takes $25\frac{8}{10}$ grains of gold to make a dollar according to law. Now the law cannot be supposed to mean that $16\frac{67}{100}$ grains of gold shall be equal in value to $25\frac{8}{10}$ grains of gold, although this inference follows from the above facts, according to the axiom that two things equal to the same thing are equal to each other; hence we must seek some other interpretation of the law consistent with common sense.

It may perhaps be said that the intention of the law is to make these coinages of equal money force, irrespective of value. If this is so, how is the intention of the law to be carried out? Money force is value in exchange for commodities; value in payment of debt. If it were not for the coercion of the law, $412\frac{1}{2}$ grains of silver could not possibly have the same money force at the present time as $25\frac{8}{10}$ grains of gold; therefore, money force conferred by law must be something different from the money force that attaches to value. If the law, therefore, is to sustain these two quantities of metal, respectively, at the same money force, it must be done by modifying the natural money force as measured by their intrinsic value.

There are only three conceivable ways of accomplishing this, namely:

1st. Adding to the deficient intrinsic value of

the silver enough legal force to bring it up to the intrinsic value of the gold.

2d. Using legal force to neutralize so much of the intrinsic value of the gold as is in excess of the intrinsic value of the silver; or—

3d. By applying legal force to both coinages, so as to raise the silver above, and reduce the gold below, its intrinsic value until they are brought to a parity.

These are obviously the only conceivable modes of effecting the alleged purpose of the law, and by an effort of abstract reasoning they may be, perhaps, equally conceivable, but they are by no means equally practicable.

If the government could impose and enforce an export duty of thirty-five per cent. on gold in every form it might force $25\frac{8}{10}$ grains of gold down in value to a parity with $412\frac{1}{2}$ grains of silver within the United States, but this cannot be done. No export duty can be imposed upon gold, because it is a product of several of the States, and the Constitution forbids export duties on the products of any State; but even if the Constitutional prohibition did not exist, the measure would prove futile, because history shows that no export duties on the precious metals can be enforced.

It may be asserted, therefore, absolutely, that there is no way in which our government can reduce the value of $25\frac{8}{10}$ grains of gold, either to an equality with $412\frac{1}{2}$ grains of silver, or to some intermediate point between their actual relative values, and, therefore, in order to carry out the intention of the law, as alleged, the $412\frac{1}{2}$ grains of silver in the standard dollar will have to be held up to the level of value of $25\frac{8}{10}$ grains of gold. We know this latter alternative is practicable, because the credit of the government is now holding the standard silver dollar up to that level, and it will probably be able to continue to do so, unless the mass of these dollars should prove ultimately too great for the sustaining force of the government's credit. Since $412\frac{1}{2}$ grains of silver are worth to-day only $16\frac{67}{100}$ grains of gold, the legal force added to this value to bring the money force of the standard silver dollar up to $25\frac{8}{10}$ grains, is precisely equivalent to $9\frac{13}{100}$ of gold. Take away this legal force and the standard silver dollar will have only its value force, which is $16\frac{67}{100}$ grains of gold.

This coinage of the standard silver dollar by the government is a new departure in finance. It was begun as a substitute for the free coinage of silver, when the ratio between the value of gold and silver on the market, though but little different from the ratio of value affixed to the coins by law, was nevertheless sufficient to render the continued free coinage of silver equivalent to debasing the monetary unit; but since the law of February, 1878, was passed, the ratio has widened very materially, so that to-day the government is discharging its debts and paying its officials, its soldiers, its pensioners, its clerks, and its laborers, in standard dollar coins (or certificates representing such coins). These contain each a quantity of silver that has cost the government only from $\frac{65}{100}$ to $\frac{80}{100}$ of a gold dollar. As long as the persons who receive this money directly from the Treasury can pass it off at the legal appraisement, they will lose nothing; nor will any person handling these coins and certificates suffer loss as long as the government holds their money force up to the gold standard; but if this upholding by the government should cease, and if, in consequence of the loss of that support, the money force of the standard silver dollar should drop to its intrinsic value only, it is absolutely certain that every such dollar will immediately lose 35 cents of purchasing force, making a loss of 35 per cent. on the whole silver dollar coinage. This loss will fall primarily upon those who happen at that time to have the coins in their possession, and the government will be justly chargeable with the loss.

Unless the government maintains these coins at the value at which they have been paid out at the Treasury, it will be guilty of dishonesty, for the standard silver dollars have been coined out of bullion costing the government much less than the face value of the coins, while the government realized their full face value when they were paid out for wages, salaries, and pensions, or in settlement for other full gold value received by the government.

The government, therefore, has no right to withdraw from these coins the sustaining force of its credit; it is bound to the people at large to redeem every standard dollar with $25\frac{8}{10}$ grains of gold, just as it is bound to redeem the greenbacks in that way. It would no more be justified in leaving the holders of the standard dollars with only the bullion value of $412\frac{1}{2}$ grains of silver to show for the honest dollar's worth of labor, or other value given in exchange for that dollar, than it would be if it left the holders of the greenbacks to realize what they could out of the paper and ink that constitutes their material. The explicit promise to pay the greenbacks in coin is not more binding upon the government than is the moral obligation to redeem the standard silver dollars in gold if gold should come to be the only money fully up to that "unit of value" which was established by the general coinage law.*

Another result of the silver coins dropping to their bullion value will be that all buying and selling will be done on the basis of the standard silver dollars, and the gold coins will cease to be money and become merchandise only. As it is computed that the gold coins now in this country amount in the aggregate to $650,000,000, their

* If any unavoidable circumstance should cause the standard silver dollars to decline in current value, *i.e.*, in money force, to their bullion value, that is, to lose thirty-five per cent. of their purchasing power, the government would be bound in good faith to restore them to full value by redeeming them in gold as soon as practicable.

demonetization will contract our total supply of money by just that amount. The consequences of such a contraction must be disastrous to all, but this is not the place to discuss them.

The only way in which the government can maintain its silver and gold coins at a parity of purchasing force is by such administrative measures as will enable anyone at any time to exchange gold for silver or silver for gold. If provision for this is made, and if the resources of the government are believed by the public to be sufficient for the purpose, no one will discriminate between the two metals in his private transactions, and the equilibrium of their purchasing force will not be disturbed. In this case the principles explained in the Chapter on Confidence as a Basis of Money (Chapter VII.), again assert themselves. The government must be able to protect the coins of the cheaper metal against a lapse to their bullion value, it must take adequate measures to do so, and above all, the people must believe that the government is both able and resolved to maintain the coinages in equilibrium.

Upon this view it is obvious that the public confidence in the purposes of the government will not alone suffice. Confidence in its ability must also pervade the people. Now, confidence in the ability of the government to accomplish this purpose will be strengthened or weakened according to the estimate formed by the public of the strain to which the government's gold resources are subjected, as compared with the volume and availability of those resources. Manifestly, if the mass of silver dollars and of coin notes based on silver bullion continues to increase, without corresponding additions to the stock of gold in the Treasury, the public will grow more and more apprehensive, and there must inevitably come a time when some will lose confidence and begin to hoard gold. If these hoarders should become numerous there would soon be a run on the Treasury for gold, while its receipts would be almost exclusively in silver.

Then would come the test. If all demands on the Treasury for gold should be met, and no objection be made to receiving silver, confidence may be restored, but any wavering on either point would end the struggle. Gold would cease to be money in the United States, and our great republic would be debased to the monetary level of Asia, Africa, and South and Central America. No one can tell in advance when confidence is going to be shaken; no one foresaw the panics of 1873, 1884, and 1890; but all men of business experience know that the Treasury is already heavily weighted and that just now nothing can be safer than to stop the silver purchases.

CHAPTER XIII.

PAPER MONEY

From what precedes it is apparent that to the people of an industrial community it is essential that all their money should be of such material, and so rooted in natural laws, as to merit and to obtain universal confidence, both as a medium of exchange and as a measure of value. For this reason many economists insist that the law should recognize nothing as money but coins of gold, silver, or copper, because these alone possess intrinsically, and in the highest degree, the qualities which experience has shown to be characteristic of good money. It is to be considered, however, that a great volume of circulation, consisting exclusively of these metals, is a very costly appliance, and though the cost of carrying it may be widely distributed, still it cannot be escaped, and must be very sensibly felt as a burden upon all the industries of the country.

In order to appreciate the force of this objection to an exclusively metallic circulation, we need, first of all, to fully realize that every dollar of money actually present in any community belongs to some individual or institution, and that every such dollar is inert capital, void of increase and earning nothing. Whether carried in the pocket or locked in a safe, every coin and every note costs to its possessor, day by day, the loss of whatever interest or profit he might obtain by parting with it, through investing its value in some productive form, *i.e.*, in a savings bank deposit or in bonds, stocks, promissory notes, real estate, machinery, tools, animals, etc. All these and many other forms of property yield to their possessor either profit or pleasure without diminution of their value as property; but money yields nothing while it is kept. To derive pleasure or profit from money one must part with it.

While it is true that money is a burden to those who keep it, still, since everybody requires to use money at some time or another and many have to use it continually, there is always a great deal of money necessarily kept awaiting use; but every person so keeping it, and every bank or other institution keeping money on hand, bears a proportionate share of the burden of its idleness. That this is felt to be a burden, is manifest by the actions of individuals and banks respecting it. Every person who has money paid to him in an amount greater than he has immediate need to keep in hand, goes about to rid himself of the surplus by depositing it in a bank, or by buying something, or by lending to his neighbor, in one form or another. Merchants, traders, and manufacturers keep as little cash on hand as possible, even though they possess large capital; while the great operators in exchange, securities and produce habitually draw their bank balances down to the lowest point they consider consistent with safety to their business, and if, at the end of any day's operations, one of these finds his balance larger than necessary, he will try to lend out the excess, even at a very low rate of interest.

So great is the burden of idle money that in many kinds of business needing the use of money for short periods of time only, it is found more economical to borrow for such periods than to hold so much money over the intervening spaces of time; thus, builders are always large borrowers, farmers invariably get advances on a maturing crop; while factors, warehousemen, and others engaged in marketing agricultural products would have their commissions and profits consumed in loss of interest if they should undertake to keep idle all through the late spring and the summer the money they know they must pay out during the autumn and winter. The uniformity of practice in this respect among business men is incontestable evidence that it is to the material interest of each individual to act in that way; and since communities consist wholly of individuals, the same rule of conduct must be regarded as also advantageous to the community; hence it is evident that no community willingly or knowingly burdens itself with more money than it needs.

Poor communities, like men of small means, cannot afford to keep even the least amount they are constantly having need for, hence they depend upon borrowing, and it is common, within limited circles, to economize the use of money as much as possible by direct exchange of services and products, one with another. The same thing occurs in communities that are not poor, but where neighbors know each other and have confidence one in another, as is seen in farming localities and in some old towns and villages. It is generally said in such cases that money is scarce, but it is not generally understood that the scarcity is due to economy, not to poverty. Currency is scarce in such communities for the same reason that horses are scarce in Venice and wherever else their use can be dispensed with. Idle money is as expensive as an idle horse.

A community that produces neither gold nor silver can obtain these only by importation, in exchange for the products of its labor, and to whatever extent they are imported, to the same extent must there be a reduction in the importations of food, clothing, raw material, and other commodities that can be industrially utilized and so made a source of future profit. Even in places where the mining of the precious metals is the chief occupation of the population, no more of the product of the mines is retained than barely suffices for the local circulation, it being necessary for the maintenance of the community to exchange the greater part for articles available for its sustenance and comfort.

Having fully realized that the entire volume of circulation in any community is a burden upon its industries, it is next in order to inquire how that burden may be lightened, and the answer will be found to be, first, by abstaining from legislation tending to enlarge the circulation beyond actual needs; and, secondly, by using paper money to a greater or less extent. The first point will be treated in the chapter entitled Volume of Circulation; the second is to be now established.

Of course the burden of idle money is the same whether such money be of metal or paper, but a part of the cost of "carrying" paper money is offset by the profit upon its issue, while there is no such offset in the case of coins. Banks issue their own notes in exchange for interest-bearing obligations of some character, and as long as those notes remain "out" the bank has the use of that capital free of cost. The profit from such use coming to the bank is (taking the bank and the rest of the community as one whole) an offset to the loss of profit upon the same amount of capital which has been sustained by the members of the community who have, for the same period of time, been successively holding the notes. The first cost of the notes to the bank which issues them is small; but if the bank had no power to issue notes, and was compelled, before it could discount paper, to buy bullion and get it coined, the cost of the bullion would be only a fraction less than the money produced by its mintage. The saving to the community, therefore, from the use of paper money is about equal to the annual interest on the volume of such money less the expense of its issue, redemption, and maintenance in a clean condition. This saving is less upon government issues of currency than upon bank notes, because, the expenses being the same in both cases, the gross saving on government paper money is merely the interest upon an equal amount of its funded debt, while the saving on bank issues is the interest on an equal amount of commercial debt, and the rate of interest on government debts is always less than the rate charged for bank loans.

Owing to the considerations here noted, and to others which will be hereafter referred to, paper money has come largely into use in modern times; and wherever the conditions of industry, credit, law, and social life are such as to admit of the general circulation of paper money its use has been found to be both economical and convenient. The employment of paper money had its origin in the use of bills of exchange, which are paper orders for money issued for money deposited at one place and redeemable at another place in money of equivalent value; a device which naturally suggested a similar device, enabling merchants to deposit money at one time and draw it out at another. Manifestly a bill of exchange would be a bank-note if it were made redeemable at the place of its issue.

Bank-notes came into use in Italy during the twelfth century, and their use afterward followed the development of trade in the several countries of modern Europe.* Like the use of bills of exchange, the circulation of bank-notes rests entirely upon the credit enjoyed by the issuing banks; but this fundamental principle was for centuries either unperceived or disregarded by certain governments, which, observing the favor enjoyed by bank-notes, conceived the idea of augmenting their resources by issues of paper money with no basis but the force of the royal mandate. This force was at first applied to existing bank currencies, and variously. In some cases the government took forcibly from the bank the treasure held against its note issues, in other cases the government borrowed the treasure; but in both cases the institutions were released from obligation to redeem the notes, and, in extreme instances, laws were made forbidding any subject to refuse the notes in payment for debts, property, produce or labor. Sometimes loans to the government were made by additional issues of notes, without adding to the treasure behind them (this would now be called watering the circulation), and sometimes the government debt to the bank

* See American Encyclopædia, vol. vii., p. 363.

constituted the original and sole basis of the note issues. In course of time governments came to issue paper money directly (dispensing with banks), and such issues have been conspicuous among the factors deciding momentous crises in history.

From this sketch it appears that paper money is of two kinds: that issued by banks and that issued by governments, and further examination will show that each of these two kinds may be classified into convertible and inconvertible. Convertible paper money is that which is maintained at a parity of value with metallic money, by means of arrangements giving to the public the right and the means to convert the notes, at will, into equivalent amounts in coin. Inconvertible paper money is that in respect to which no such arrangements exist. Three conditions are essential to maintaining the convertibility of paper money, viz.:

1. The existence of a monetary unit, established by law, or so rooted in the traditions and habits of the people as to be practically beyond chance of variation.

2. Adequate provision for securing the conversion of notes into coin without unreasonable expense or delay, and in any amount likely to be demanded.

3. General confidence among the people in the permanency and sufficiency of the two preceding conditions.

Inconvertible paper money may be maintained in circulation by a government, but under present conditions of corporate credit it does not seem possible for any bank to maintain such a circulation. The Bank of Venice, in the twelfth century, and the Bank of Amsterdam, in the seventeenth, were able to obtain deposits not subject to withdrawal, and they long maintained this rule, but both abandoned it in time. While the rule lasted the ownership of such deposits was transferred from one person to another by means of checks or orders vouched or certified by the bank; and this presents the nearest approach to an inconvertible bank currency that history records. It evidences either extraordinary depression of general credit or great social and political disorder. There have been many instances in which banknotes have been maintained in circulation during periods of suspension, but such currencies have not been voluntarily adopted by the people; and in most cases of suspended banks the government has bolstered their circulation by receiving the notes in the payment of taxes and other public dues.

Inconvertible paper money, issued by a government, may be maintained at a parity of value with metallic money, provided the following conditions, five in number, exist:

1. There must be a monetary unit, as in the case of convertible paper money.

2. There must be a considerable volume of metallic money in the country, and sufficient foreign trade, or other specific use for coins to keep them in general circulation.

3. The government must make no distinction, in its dealings with the people, between the two kinds of money; both or either must be received and paid out with at least ostensible impartiality.

4. Provision must be made by taxation, or by voluntary funding for the prompt absorption of any redundancy apparent in the volume of outstanding paper money.

5. The people using the paper money must have confidence in the purpose and the ability of the government to maintain indefinitely the four preceding conditions.

Both convertible and inconvertible paper money become depreciated the moment public confidence is shaken in the purpose or power of the issuer to preserve the conditions under which alone such money can circulate in interchangeable effectiveness with coins. Under Gresham's law the primary effect of the depreciation is to cause contraction of the total volume of circulating medium, by expelling from it all money that is not depreciated. What is left thus becomes a sort of leprous currency, with which association and mingling is abhorrent to all forms of sound and healthy money.

A community abandoned to a depreciated currency suffers incalculable loss, both materially and morally, proofs of which are afforded by general history, but they abound in the annals of our own country where both before and just after the

Revolution almost every Colony and State tried the experiment of paper money and suffered from its depreciation. The people of the late Confederate States suffered enormously. Against the economy and convenience of paper money, therefore, we must set its liability to depreciation, and before any satisfactory conclusion can be reached we must consider separately the two kinds of paper money, viz., that issued by the government and that issued by the banks—endeavoring to ascertain on the one hand their relative cheapness and convenience, and on the other their relative liability to depreciation. These questions are treated in the two succeeding chapters.

CHAPTER XIV.

TREASURY-NOTE OR DUE-BILL CIRCULATION

The power to prescribe what shall be legal tender for debt must not be confounded with the natural right possessed by every sovereign government to determine what shall be the medium for paying public dues. That right flows from the right of taxation, and were the States of the Union not prohibited by the Federal Constitution from issuing bills of credit, there would be no force in the legal tender inhibition to restrain them from maintaining a State currency receivable for State dues.*

* The United States Supreme Court has lately decided anew that the matured coupons of State bonds are a valid tender for dues to that State, hence there can be no doubt that a State has a natural right to issue obligations of its own, and to give them currency, by engaging to receive them in payment of taxes and other dues.

So may a large property owner or capitalist maintain a circulation of his own due-bills, by making them good for the payment of rent and other dues to him.

In the Constitution, however, the States have surrendered this natural right, as far as bills of credit go, and therefore, as in the case of legal tender, the Federal government alone may exercise it as the common agent and organ of all the States for these functions.

The principle upon which an irredeemable due-bill currency rests, is worthy of careful observation, because it is one of the fundamental principles underlying all monetary circulation except that of the precious metals. It is well illustrated by the circulation of blood in the human body, of which Harvey's celebrated exposition may be abbreviated as follows:

The muscular force of the heart keeps pumping the blood in a continuous, bright red stream through the arteries, which, at first great ducts, diminish in diameter and divide into smaller pipes as they extend toward the surfaces they are to nourish; upon these surfaces the attenuated arteries are spread out, a tangle of innumerable hair-like tubes, where at length the propelling force of the heart is spent, and where, changed in color from scarlet to purple, the fluid moves languidly to its myriad points of ultimate circulation. From each of these points the blood is sent back toward the source of its emission by pulsating movements in the veins, which, beginning at the capillaries, urge it with increasing energy through conduits continually enlarging in diameter as they diminish in number, until it is poured into the heart a single torrent, black with the impurities of the system. Thence the stream runs through the lungs, where it is filtered and cleansed and returning to the heart is sent forth again on its ceaseless round, the volume and the essential composition of the fluid remaining always the same.

A due-bill or Treasury-note circulation may become, like the blood, an ever-flowing stream, and it may be maintained undepreciated, even though the notes are irredeemable, and, therefore, never convertible into coin, provided the Treasury, like the heart, draws back from the channels of circulation all that it puts out. When the energy of the public expenditure is sending forth an incessant stream of paper money, the force of taxation should be sufficient to draw it all back into the Treasury after it has made the circuit of society, for otherwise the channels of circulation will become gorged, and stagnant currency is as fatal to health in a monetary system as a languid circulation of the blood is to the animal organism.

Let us follow the note circulation under such a system. The officers and employees of the government, the soldiers, the contractors for public supplies, the mail carriers, the artisans and laborers on public works, with many others, receive the fresh issues as they come crisp from the Treasury. All these persons use the notes to pay the grocer, the butcher, and other tradespeople; some part goes in servants' wages, some in travel and amusement; in one way or another the notes penetrate every nook and cranny in the community. From these innumerable points, which may be called the capillaries of money circulation, where money passes from hand to hand, the notes enter the channels of trade; they are deposited in bank one day, drawn out another, shipped from city to country, and back from country to city, until at length the tax-collector gathers them in and sends them back to the Treasury, soiled with the dust of traffic, the grime of toil, and, perhaps, even the stain of vice. From the moment of issue to that of return to the Treasury, every note passes from hand to hand, from bank to bank, from place to place, entirely because of its tax-paying force—just as every globule of blood is kept in motion by the force that tends always to hurry back to the heart those globules that have severally reached and passed the points of their ultimate circulation. Such circulation may be maintained upon two conditions: First, that taxation shall always keep pace with expenditure, so as to insure that every dollar that is put out will be ultimately demanded back in payment of taxes; and, secondly, that the stability of the government is sufficiently established to exclude all doubt as to its power to enforce the return of the currency by means of taxation.

These conditions are essential, because a currency sustained solely in this way owes its efficiency entirely to the demand for it created by the tax. Take that away and it will pass through a rapid process of depreciation or into utter discredit and worthlessness; revive its receivability for taxes, and you revive its value and restore it to circulation. The repeal of the law and the overthrow of the government equally destroy such a currency. A due-bill system, as here described, is virtually a method of borrowing by the government from the people, upon the security of the proceeds of future taxation, and without paying interest. The lenders are the employees of the government, its soldiers and sailors, the laborers it employs, the contractors and dealers from whom it purchases supplies; they lend the value of their services or their property, and the government due bills are their receipts. From these primary creditors the government I. O. U.'s pass to its only debtors, the tax-payers, who settle their taxes with the government by passing the paper back into the Treasury.

It is manifest that a government sustained through the instrumentality of an irredeemable currency is anticipating its revenues, and that it forces the most defenceless class of its citizens to lend it the means to do so. Here is another proof that it is money's worth and not money that is really the object of universal pursuit, for the government gets money's worth in labor, services, materials, and supplies, gives a receipt for them in the form of currency, and exacts from its tax-payers the redemption and return of these receipts. No device combines within itself so many of the essential ingredients of tyranny as a due-bill circulation, redeemable only in commutation for taxes; for while it represents the extreme of arbitrary exaction by the government, it fastens upon the mass of the people a yoke from which they cannot escape, except by themselves destroying the value of the paper upon which they have advanced full value by giving their services, their products, and their property in exchange for it. By submitting to the issue of such a currency the subjects of a monarchy abandon their only effective defence against oppression, and they aggravate enormously the cost of revolution, while the citizens of a free state who allow such a currency to be established among them, invest their rulers with a power dangerous to liberty and difficult of restraint. The reason is the same in both cases; an irredeemable government currency binds the people indefinitely to a scale of taxation commensurate with the volume of the paper issues, and thereafter taxation can be reduced only by contracting the currency or by suffering it to become depreciated, alternatives of which both are oppressive and of which therefore either is difficult of adoption.

A due-bill currency may or may not be made a legal tender for debt. An example on each side is afforded by our own recent history. The currency issued by the Confederate government was not made a legal tender; it was an inconvertible due-bill or Treasury-note circulation. Had its volume been adjusted to the receipts from taxes, or had taxation been raised to the scale of the currency issues, an artificial circulation could have been maintained that would have prevented depreciation up to the time when the Southern people lost faith in the result of the war, *i.e.*, when the stability of the government was seen to be in danger.

The law-makers at Richmond, however, failed to understand or to apply this principle. They shrunk from levying taxes on a scale commensurate with the needs of the government, and consequently, through the instrumentality of a baseless currency, some of the population were cozened, and others were coerced out of the needed supplies, while many escaped contributions altogether. In this way the ultimate cost to the people was vastly greater than it would have been if the value realized by the government had been taken in the orderly manner in which taxes are collected, while the wrong and injustice to the defenceless classes were immense and irremediable. To the destruction of war there were thus added the sickening miseries of a depreciated currency.

If there are in the world to-day any people who ought to appreciate the blessings of sound money and stable values, they are the people of those States of the Union which are still suffering, after more than a quarter of a century, from the effects of a currency that was neither sound in principle nor stable in value. The direst losses of the war at the South were in human life and human happiness, which, though irretrievable, fell only on the generations fairly subject to them. The entire people suffered greatly also in material comfort because profitable industry everywhere was interrupted and commerce was curtailed; serious disasters, but such as a country of varied and abounding resources would soon have recovered from; but the Confederate currency carried impoverishment and demoralization into every corner of the land; it threw upon the aged, the infirm, the women, and even upon generations then unborn, the vast burden of the war expenditure, and what is far worse, it fostered extravagance, dishonesty, speculation, and gambling; it sucked up the accumulated earnings of generations of honest toilers and transferred, first, their securities, and, sometimes, ultimately, their lands and homesteads to the few who proved astute enough both to avoid military service and to take advantage of the general confusion and distress, to their own enrichment.

The Government of the United States, in 1862, issued an irredeemable paper currency, commonly called greenbacks, and made the notes a legal tender for debts. In this case, as in that of the Confederate currency, taxation was not adjusted to the volume of currency emission, consequently the greenbacks became depreciated, although throughout the North commerce and manufactures were enormously stimulated by the war; the country suffered little or nothing from invasion, and immigration was constantly bringing in resources from outside. One incident in the history of the greenbacks is highly instructive, as showing, first, that the effectiveness of money depends upon its "passing;" and, second, that its ultimate availability in trade settlements will cause any given money to "pass" everywhere within the area covered by such settlements.

Of course the first issues of greenbacks went to pay the army and the government officers and clerks, and for a time they sufficed for these purposes; but after a while it was observed that the channels of circulation within which the new currency flowed were few and narrow, and, moreover, they were getting filled up. The banks refused to receive the notes on deposit or to accept them in payment of maturing paper, and, although they were a legal tender, merchants and other business men having paper payable in bank were restrained by conventional opinion from tendering payment in greenbacks. Some persons were prompted by this and other financial embarrassments in which the government became involved to propose the organization of national banks, and Mr. Chase incorporated into the legislation a provision requiring the national banks to redeem their own notes in greenbacks.

This requirement proved to be effective in giving currency to the greenbacks, for of course the banks eagerly accepted a scheme which made it a patriotic thing for them to put out a great circulation which they were not only allowed but almost, one may say, fantastically compelled, to redeem in a medium constantly depreciating in value, while they had their own means invested in government bonds, payable, principal and interest, in gold, and lest, through density of intellect, any bank officers and directors should be tempted or deluded into letting go such a good thing, the bonds themselves were locked in the Treasury at Washington!

Yet Mr. Chase is entitled to credit for a brilliant success in financiering, for the government was relieved, the banks were enriched, and everybody applauded. Who paid? The People—it is always The People who pay. They paid in the increased cost of the war, in the deplorable moral effect of a depreciated currency, in all the chicanery and depravity flowing from the gambling in gold and stocks that prevailed from 1862 to 1879, in the corruption that ravened and exulted at every seat of government from Washington to the smallest municipality, in the long and exhausting process preceding the resumption of specie payments in 1879, and in the present perilous condition of the currency, due largely to the fallacies bred among the people by the false position in which greenbacks were placed, and still are held, by legislative force alone—a false position, made all the more pernicious in its influence by the subsequent sanction given to it by the Supreme Court of the United States.

CHAPTER XV.

BANK-NOTE CIRCULATION

In the chapter on Paper Money it was shown that two kinds of such money have been in use at various times and places, viz., government currency and bank-notes. We have considered the subject of government currency, we come now to that of bank-notes. In order to keep our ideas clear on this subject it is necessary to exclude from consideration here currencies which, though issued by banks, have been, as it were, fathered by the government; but, in applying this exclusion, distinction must be made between the wholesome regulation and restraint, which all governments are justified in imposing by law upon the issue of bank-notes and the adoption of such notes as a government currency in return for, or in consideration of, accommodation or advantages supplied to the government by the issuing banks. The excluded currencies are of a mixed character, partly governmental due-bills, partly bank-notes, and they will receive consideration hereafter in connection with the present National Bank circu-

BANK-NOTE CIRCULATION

lation, which is a type of the whole class. Our attention now should be confined to bank-note circulation proper, a purely commercial device called into existence by industrial and social convenience, and maintained wholly through the uncoerced confidence of the people who use such notes as their money.

It has been shown (Chapter XIII.) that bills of exchange were the first paper money, and that bank-notes were afterward devised. Checks on banks of deposit, so familiar to us, are the most recent development of the bill of exchange, and when "certified" they acquire also the force of a bank-note. Indeed, these certified checks are very much like the earliest bank-notes, which were merely certificates of deposit invented to economize the use of the precious metals. It would be quite practicable now for depositors to draw checks in round sums of five, ten, etc., dollars, payable to bearer, have them certified by a bank, and (unless Section 3413, United States Revised Statutes should be construed as prohibiting it) use them as bank-notes. Should such certified checks obtain general currency they would become money in the community where so circulating, and would differ from all other kinds of money now in use in this country in being simply a creation of credit, unsupported by governmental provision, and dependent for the continuity of their use wholly on their acceptability to the public.

Such certified checks, used as money, would be,

for all practical purposes, like the bank-notes that were in circulation prior to 1862, and the supposed process of their issue illustrates how those bank-notes were issued. During the older period the banks that issued notes placed them in circulation by paying them out upon the checks of their depositors, while under the system above imagined the checks themselves would be certified. This illustration of the certified check is intended only to make quite plain the true nature of the bank-note by showing that such checks, should they be used for money, would serve all the purposes of bank-notes.

The main advantage to be derived by any community from banks of issue consists, first, in the economy of paper as compared with metallic money; and, secondly, in the utility of such banks to productive industry. The plea of economy for the use of paper money, rather than coin, applies to government issues as well as bank-notes, the only difference being in the relative saving effected, and this difference has been shown to be in favor of the bank-note. It should be observed, too, that it is fallacious to claim, as some do, that a government currency, though the less economical of the two, is better for the people at large, inasmuch as the saving effected in the interest disbursements of the government tends to the benefit of all the people, while the profit derived from the issue of notes goes to the bank and its stockholders. It may be true that the use of a government currency tends to lower the rate of interest on government bonds, but the share of any one citizen in a fractional saving of interest by the government is so infinitesimal as to be practically worthless, while, on the other hand, it is certainly true that the increase of bank-note issues tends to reduce the rate of interest on commercial loans, and the reduction of one or two per cent. per annum in the rate of interest on the loans made by banks to their customers is a matter of immense consequence to all borrowers, and, consequently, of such great advantage to all industries as to be incalculably more beneficial to the masses than any saving in interest by the government. It especially relieves those classes of the community most burdened by the cost of carrying its stock of money.

In the United States, where the government taxation is not in the least degree affected by the interest on the public debt, the people gain absolutely nothing from the greenback currency, amounting to $346,000,000; while the issue of bank-notes to that amount based, not on bonds but on commercial paper, would probably make seven per cent. a maximum rate of interest throughout all our agricultural communities, except those in the newest States and the Territories, and would even there greatly reduce present rates for money. Under the imperfect and often hazardous system of note issues by State banks between 1820 and 1860, the prevailing rates during that period in the communities where those banks were located were six per cent. for discounts, and seven per cent. for interest.

The history of the Bank of Stockholm affords a striking proof of the effect of bank issues of currency in reducing the rates of interest. This institution was established early in the seventeenth century by a merchant, and subsequently, viz., in 1688, was made a State bank. At that date, as one of the conditions of the change, it was limited to eight per cent. as the maximum rate for loans on good security, and it was required to allow six per cent. interest on all deposits, except those of the government, which drew no interest. As a consequence of its operations and its growing credit, the rates of interest rapidly declined throughout the kingdom, and before the close of the century the bank rate for loans was successively reduced to seven, six, four, and finally to three per cent. per annum, while the rate allowed to depositors was reduced, *pari passu*, until it reached two per cent.

It is obvious that during those twelve years the people of Sweden gained from cheaper money vastly more than they could have gained from any saving in the interest on the public debt that could possibly have been effected by issues of government currency, and they would have been greatly injured if such government currency had been maintained in circulation by the prohibition of bank-notes—the policy pursued by the United

States since February, 1862. I say this has been our policy, because the National Bank notes are truly a government currency and possess none of the essentials of bank-notes. When the system was first instituted the National Banks were able to make large profits, because they were getting six per cent. interest on the bonds, besides having the use, free of interest, of money amounting to very nearly ninety per cent. of that invested in the bonds. These profits, however, were not such as banks of issue make on their circulation, as is proved by the fact that there is no profit on the circulation at present, whereas if they had been profits made on circulation, they would have been about the same during every year of average business prosperity. There is no profit now on circulation simply because at present the bonds cost one hundred and fifteen per cent., yielding as an investment only about two and one-half per cent., while the circulation (less redemption fund) is only $\frac{85}{115}$, or under seventy-five per cent. of the outlay for bonds. The profits of the earlier period were such as accrued because the banks bought their bonds for about ten per cent. cash and ninety per cent. credit without having to pay interest on the credit portion of such cost, although they received interest on the face of the bonds.

Because there was no profit in it, the circulation of the National Banks never did make money cheap to borrowers. The issue of notes upon bonds was a bonus given to the banks by the government in order to secure their aid in effecting two objects of vital importance, viz.: First, to relieve the stagnation in greenback circulation; and, secondly, to enlarge the market for government bonds. Of these two objects the first was effected by making National Bank notes redeemable in greenbacks, which, of course, encouraged the banks to receive the latter on deposit, to which they had previously been averse, and the second was effected by putting it in the power of the banks to borrow back from the people, without interest, very nearly all the money they were lending to the government at high rates of interest.

It is just as true in economics as it is in physics that a given force can produce only its appropriate measure of effect, and the corollary of this theorem is also true in both sciences, viz., that you cannot infer a latent effect when the obvious effect exhausts the full efficiency of the force. Applying these principles to the present case, it must be conceded that the risk taken by the banks during the war, in buying bonds and banking on greenbacks, were fully commensurate with any profits made out of the arrangement for circulation then or afterward, hence there is no basis for assuming that these profits produced any effect in reducing rates of interest on commercial loans, while all the evidence is to the contrary. The profits described having long since ceased, of course they cannot now have any such effect, hence the National Bank currency never has possessed one of the essential qualities of a true bank-note circulation, viz., that of cheapening loans.*

That notes issued against deposited bonds never can tend to the cheapening of loans will be evident when it is considered that such notes de-

---

* The relation of the National Banks to the currency is very imperfectly understood generally, and by many persons it is wholly misunderstood.

The fact is, the "National Currency," which is the legal designation of the circulating notes bearing the names of different National Banks, is not in any true sense of the term a bank-note circulation. These notes are issued by the government to the banks only after the bank has deposited in the Treasury United States bonds exceeding in value the notes to be issued, which bonds are required by law to be held as security for the redemption of the notes. The bank in its turn issues these notes to the public, and thus guarantees their ultimate payment, besides undertaking, if called upon to do so, to furnish greenbacks in exchange for any part of the issue.

Before a National Bank can "take out" $9,000 of circulation, it must deposit interest-bearing bonds to the par value of $10,000, and as soon as it "puts out" the $9,000 in notes, it must deposit $450 in greenbacks in the Treasury, as a fund for current redemptions. Thereafter these notes, amounting to $9,000, are mingled in the general currency of the country; the bank cannot call them in if it would, and nobody ever thinks of bringing any of them to the bank for redemption. If they are destroyed, the government is released from their payment, but the bank cannot withdraw its bonds until it makes a deposit as for their redemption.

When regarded practically, the arrangements as to the national currency are found to work as follows:

A new bank is to be formed in some country town, and the enterprising men who unite to get it up withdraw a portion of the capital they have invested in their business, convert it into money, and so establish the bank. Say that together they have $100,000 paid in. It is clear that if each man had kept his share of that $100,000, and used it in his business, the town would have

rive their existence from the deposit of the bonds and their value from that of the bonds; they are issued *to* the bank really, not *by* it, and while in its possession are a part of its assets, being col-

had the benefit of the whole sum, employed locally, but the National Bank laws require that a bank of $100,000 capital shall deposit $25,000 of bonds at par, while they permit the bank to get on those bonds only $22,500 in circulating notes.

If the subscribers to the new bank hold among them the $25,000 of bonds, then the $22,500 of circulation would be an addition to the local supply of currency of just that amount; but as is almost invariably the case if the bank has to send to Chicago or New York or Boston to buy its bonds, then the very first step toward its organization takes away from the place the amount of currency required to effect the purchase; for four per cent. bonds it would take away $28,650, so that, even after getting back $22,500 in circulating notes issued to the new bank, the community would still be deprived of the use of over $6,000.

It thus appears that every increase in the circulation of a National Bank transfers loanable funds from the place where the bank is located to the place at which it buys its bonds; and conversely, every time a National Bank reduces or surrenders its circulation, loanable funds are transferred back from the place where its bonds are sold to the place where the bank does its business.

The scarcity and the high price of bonds have practically concentrated them in a few places. New York is perhaps the only place where there is anything like a regular market for these bonds, and therefore, speaking broadly, it may be said that the increase of National Bank circulation transfers loanable funds from the country to New York, and the reduction of National Bank circulation re-transfers those funds from New York to points in the country.

It will be seen, of course, that these effects of contraction and expansion in the volume of the national currency are precisely opposite to the effects produced by similar variations in the volume of a true bank-note currency.

lectively representative of the bonds, its property, deposited at Washington. The notes issued to each National Bank are, indeed, government money advanced on the bank's bonds, and for all money purposes they are just like the notes issued to any other bank; the bank whose name they bear gains nothing by their prolonged circulation. Not so with bank-notes proper which are issued *by* the bank, have no vitality until issued, and cease to have any money force the moment they come back to the bank that issued them.

Unlike the National Banks, under present laws and conditions, true banks of issue have an interest in putting out all the circulation possible, and in keeping it out as long as possible, and this tends to the cheapening of loans in two ways.

First. The discount of paper and the making of loans constitute the only way in which a bank can get out circulation; hence, as between a bank desiring to extend its circulation and one confined to the use of coin or government currency in making loans, it is obvious that the bank of issue has the greater incentive to lend and can afford to take lower rates of interest than the other. Let us suppose two such banks newly established in a place where prevailing rates of interest have been six per cent. The non-issuing bank finds no inducement to lend below that rate, but the issuing bank, reckoning the profit on its circulation as equivalent to, say two per cent. per annum, can afford to lend as low as four per cent. Even if we assume that the government currency yields to the government two per cent. profit, there is no means by which borrowers can derive any benefit from that; but when banks of issue get such a profit, competition quickly and invariably forces them to divide it with those who borrow of them, because these, and these only, by their co-operation render it practicable for the bank to get its notes into circulation.

The second way in which, when banks are allowed to issue notes, rates of interest are brought lower than they are when the circulation consists wholly of coins and government currency, is through an elasticity in the volume of bank issues, which has no counterpart in the other system. Banks of issue may expand their circulation as the demand for accommodation expands, the rate of expansion being limited only by the ratio of increase in the reserve held to secure the redemption of the notes on demand. A specie reserve of one dollar to every three or four dollars of circulation has generally been accepted as sufficient to insure the complete efficiency of bank-note circulation; hence, when there is an active demand for money, the bank of issue that gets in $1,000 in specie may issue against it $3,000 or $4,000 of notes, whereas under present conditions no bank can lend out more than the $1,000 it has taken in and National Banks may lend only $750 or $850, according to location.

This power to expand the circulation very materially modifies the effect of the forces which operate from time to time to enhance the rate of interest, and if the banks authorized to issue notes are numerous, widely dispersed, and subjected to proper regulations and restraints as to such issues, they cannot fail to be always competing to put out loans, because they will be under the strongest solicitations of selfish advantage to do so, and such competition must cheapen rates of interest.

It must not be forgotten, however, that the power to put out four dollars of notes for one dollar of specie acquired is inseparable from the obligation to retire four dollars of the bank's circulation for every specie dollar withdrawn from its vaults; hence the importance of numbers, wide distribution, and intelligent effective regulation. Numbers and wide distribution are sufficient to discourage and to defeat efforts at withdrawals of specie for the purpose of producing monetary stringency through enforced contraction, for it is evident that no such effort would promise success with six thousand banks of issue scattered all over the United States, distributed as our National and State Banks are and enjoying a like degree of credit. There could hardly be any conceivable contingency in which the circulation of all these banks would simultaneously stand at the maximum proportion to coin reserve, while under ordinary circumstances it is impossible but that many would have available a margin for expansion equal to any probable contraction brought about by manipulation of a few. This safeguard could be assured if a small tax were laid upon circulation, computed upon the amounts outstanding at the end of each month, for that would operate as an inducement to banks not to keep out issues in excess of the demand for loans at fair rates of interest.

All periods of monetary stringency have followed periods of ease and cheap money; indeed they are produced by the recoil of the over-borrowing and over-trading which are fostered by cheap money, hence as a means to prevent the periodical recurrence of stringency and panic a proper system of bank-note circulation possesses some advantages of an important character. With our currency, as at present constituted, every dollar withdrawn from circulation counts against borrowers everywhere, and there is no provision for a compensating expansion of issues anywhere. The force of this will more fully appear when it is remembered that rates of interest are prices of loans, and that, like all other prices, they must vary with the varying relations between demand and supply; that is to say, when the supply of loanable funds exceeds the demand for loans, rates of interest decline; when demand exceeds supply, rates of interest rise. Now, under a system of bank-note circulation, the volume of the currency changes automatically with changes in rates of interest, hence under such a system there is a constant tendency toward steadiness both in rates of interest and in volume of currency.

It is, however, in the performance of that primary function of money, which consists in effecting industrial and commercial exchanges that a bank currency is chiefly superior to a currency of coin and government paper, singly or mixed. It may be admitted, with certain reservations not pertinent to the present question, that under normal conditions bank-notes and Treasury due-bills are equally available for measuring, and thus comparing, contemporary values, and to that extent they are equally efficient in promoting the exchange of industrial products; but to accomplish such exchanges something more is requisite than a comparison of values, and that is the actual presence of money sufficient for the liquidations involved in the series of transactions by which one group of products is exchanged for another.

Take, for example, the series of exchanges by which a farmer's crop of wheat becomes converted into fuel, lumber, horses, vehicles, tools, furniture, groceries, clothing, schooling for his children, religious comfort, medical attendance, travelling expenses, etc. At every step in this series some money must pass from one person to another, and in order that there may be neither obstruction nor friction there must be money available at the time and place of each transaction. Now when the only money in circulation is in the form of coins or government certificates for coins, or Treasury notes, the entire volume of the country's currency is more or less fixed as to its total amount, and for the reason explained in Chapter XIII. it becomes distributed from time to time according to relative employment for it in different parts of the country. In that chapter it was pointed out that idle money being a burden, no individual and no community keeps it; hence, since purely agricultural communities use very little money during long periods of each year, very little is retained there. On the other hand, when crops ripen and have to be harvested and marketed, a great deal of money is required in those communities, and, as it is not present, it must be brought there, and that involves delay, expense, and sometimes inability to command a sufficient supply.

Now no augmentation, gradual or spasmodic, in government issues of currency or in Treasury disbursements of surplus revenue, can obviate this inconvenience and expense to farmers, because a currency abundant even to the point of redundancy never overflows into places where there is no profitable employment for money, but the excess becomes absorbed in speculation, and that is carried on, not on farms but in cities. On the other hand, banks of issue, located in agricultural sections, are admirably adapted to supplying with their issues of notes these annual and comparatively brief periods of demand for money for moving the crops, and farmers whose needs are thus supplied are neither subjected to heavy discounts on the drafts drawn against their produce nor delayed in marketing their crops, or in making their purchases, by the want of money.

Under our present system of currency, during the months from March to August, the bulk of the circulating medium is finding its way, at much expense for expressage, and much cost in loss of interest, from thousands of points all over the country to the cities, and ultimately it becomes concentrated at a few centres; then, during September, October, and November, it has to be redistributed, at like expense, whereas if our six thousand banks were allowed to issue notes, as the State banks did before 1862, a great part of this trouble and expense would be avoided.

If country banks were required to keep a reserve of twenty per cent. against their note issues their entire autumnal expansion would cost just one-fifth of what it now costs to fetch currency, and, under a proper system of redemption centres, the expense could be still further curtailed. What is true of agricultural communities is equally, if less strikingly, true of every other locality where more money is needed at one season than at others, and it would, moreover, be a sensible relief to the cities and principal centres to escape the annual dumping upon them of the currency that, having performed its brief mission throughout the country, comes back to them to be "carried" until the next harvest comes around. In considering the relative utility of the two classes of banks to a population which, like ours, is wholly immersed in industry, special attention should be given to the subject of domestic exchanges, because these attend every transfer of products or commodities from one ownership or one locality to another, and they are conducted wholly by banks and bankers.

The transactions in domestic exchange have been very much cheapened by the establishment of a fixed monetary unit, and by the laws and regulations which keep all the elements of our currency constant in value and therefore interchangeable everywhere;* but the saving thus effected would be very much greater if all our National Banks were true banks of issue, for that would greatly relieve the necessity of so much of our costly "currency movements" as now consist of the outflow "to move the crops," and the return of the wave after the crops have been marketed. In some parts of the country there are four such tidal movements in the year, in others there are ordinarily only two, but with properly regulated banks of issue the necessity would pass away for any movement in excess of such transfers of specie as may be requisite to support a local expansion of bank-note issues. This would certainly reduce the expense to a third or a fourth of what it is now, and in time it would probably be reduced even below this by the retention of specie from one period to another.

We had once in this country a great many banks

* It is a mistake to attribute the cheapening of domestic exchange wholly to the National Bank currency.

chartered by the different States and authorized to issue notes payable to the bearer on demand. These notes constituted for a long time the principal currency of the country, and, notwithstanding the manifold and glaring imperfections of the system, there was virtue enough in the principle it embodied to neutralize many of the inconveniences and even dangers incident to its unregulated application. Confidence of course was essential to the circulation of the State bank-notes, for the moment anything happened to impair the public confidence in the ability of any bank to redeem its notes that moment the note-holders made "a run" for their money. It was therefore vital to banks of issue to maintain their credit, and to this end a reputation for prudent management, as well as for integrity, was essential.

A well-managed bank of issue got its notes into circulation not by buying property with them [for in that case their value would have been locked up in the property, and until the property was sold the notes could not be redeemed], but by exchanging them for the notes, drafts, or acceptances of individuals and firms engaged in business, "commercial paper" as it is called. The bank's profit was obtained in the form of discount or interest on the commercial paper, the bank-notes carrying no interest. To put out a circulation in this way was regarded as intelligent and prudent banking, if care was taken in the selection of the commercial paper "done," if the maturities of this paper corresponded with the probable course, as to time, of the bank's circulation, and if the volume of notes thus put out was adjusted to the capacity of the community to absorb currency.

Reduced to its ultimate analysis this system of banking consisted in borrowing from the public at large, without interest, the money value which the bank lent to its customers upon interest; it therefore was an exchange of corporate and financial credit for individual and commercial credit, the bank-notes issued to borrowers being eventually paid back to the bank in settlement of loans, having meanwhile circulated in the community as money.

Manifestly this kind of money is much more economically obtained than the same amount of gold and silver, consequently communities where it prevails are enabled by it to use, productively, whatever proportion of their capital they would otherwise have to keep in the unproductive form of coin.

Under such a system of banking, however, the cost of a metallic currency is not wholly avoided, because some coin has to be kept by the banks. This coin is the connecting link between the bank-note and the monetary unit, for it is the medium of redemption of the notes. Identity of value between the bank-note dollars and the monetary unit is essential both to the bank and to the holder of its notes, for the latter requires assurance as to this identity before extending his confidence to the notes, and the former is ready to furnish such assurance, because it absolutely depends upon that confidence to keep its circulation afloat. This system of banking, beginning in England, acquired its highest British development in Scotland, and grew up in this country as soon as the adoption of the Federal Constitution of 1787 and the monetary legislation of Congress established a foundation for it in the institution of metallic money and a definite and stable monetary unit.

Though there were many imperfections of system, and numerous instances of dishonest, ignorant, and imprudent management, most of the banks of issue under State charters were so managed as to materially promote the prosperity of the communities where they were established. They contributed to the wide diffusion of wealth, and they played an important part in educating the people commercially and financially, as well as in stimulating and promoting the development of our natural resources and the improvement of our methods of communication and transportation. In 1862 the National Bank Act put an end to this system of banking. If we look upon that act as simply a measure of war finance it cannot be too greatly praised, for certainly it was one of the most ingenious conceptions recorded in history, and its success places it among the highest achievements of financial ability. It is probable, however, that if the great man who conceived and established this system could to-day look upon our country, reunited and genuinely reconciled, where an enormous growth of corporate power and a dangerous concentration of wealth are coincident with the widening of those social borders, within which plodding industry sees no prospect but of an indefinite continuance of the need to plod, he would see now as clearly what are the present needs of the people as he saw their needs in 1862. That they are very different must be obvious to all who study our surroundings; that the National Bank system should now be set free to issue notes, under proper restraint and regulation, would no doubt be recognized by Mr. Chase himself.

In speaking of the banks of issue in a previous part of this chapter it was said that prudent and intelligent banking forbids a bank to endeavor to get its notes in circulation by buying property with them. This principle does not depend upon the property not being profitable to hold, or not being likely to appreciate in value, or not being readily salable, but it depends wholly upon the financial truth, established both by reason and experience, that it is not good banking to lock up a bank's funds in anything that has to be sold in the local market in order to get them out again. The only legitimate investment for the funds of a bank is the commercial paper which represents the actual industrial operations of the community, and which presumably will be paid at maturity.

No argument is necessary to prove how dependent industry is upon the convenience afforded by a market for commercial paper, nor how necessary it is that loanable capital should be encouraged to enter this market and should be protected by law in its dealings with capital productively invested; but we need to realize this dependence and this necessity in order to appreciate how important are the functions of banks in this relation, and how fundamental is the need of an effective banking system to general prosperity among the people. At present, however, we may disregard these considerations and confine our attention to the application of the principles so far established. These principles forbid a bank to invest, in any permanent form whatever, the value it borrows from the public at large upon the notes it issues payable on demand. Now the National Banks are required by law to violate this ancient and well-established rule, for while it is true that the capital, wholly or in part, is first invested in bonds, and then the notes issued upon the bonds are available for investment in commercial paper, yet the effect is the same as if the capital were held in money and the notes invested in the bonds. Take a bank with a paid-in capital of $1,000,000 and a circulation of $900,000. The effective force of such a bank as an auxiliary to productive industry should be $1,900,000, but is really less than $1,000,000, because, as the bank holds $1,000,000 in United States bonds as a basis of circulation, the bond investment locks up from $1,000,000 to $1,150,000, according to the class of bonds held, and leaves the bank only from $750,000 to $900,000 effective capital.*

Now it is manifest that practically it can be of no consequence whatever whether the amount locked up in the bonds, say generally $1,150,000, is obtained from the $1,000,000 paid in by shareholders as capital, plus the $900,000 represented by circulation, or whether it is obtained by adding to the $900,000, represented by circulation, $250,000 out of the $1,000,000 capital. Either way the public, shareholders and note-holders combined, have put into the bank $1,900,000 of money or its equivalent, and they are getting the use of only $750,000 of this sum, while under the former system they would have the use of the whole $1,900,000, while the bank would hold against it not government bonds locked up at Washington, and constantly depreciating in value, but gold and silver coin to the amount of $300,000 to $400,000, and commercial paper constantly and continuously running to maturity and amounting to $1,500,000 to $1,600,000.

Contrasting the two systems as sources of circulation, the one reduces the available money of the community from $1,000,000 to $750,000, an actual contraction of $250,000 on every million, or twenty-five per cent., while the other increases it from $1,000,000 (original capital) to $1,900,000, less

* For obvious reasons the banks generally hold four per cent. bonds, so that the larger figure is nearer the average than the smaller.

$300,000 to $400,000 coin reserved, say to $1,550,000, making an addition of fifty-five per cent. to the local supply of loanable funds.

Another feature of the National Bank system which will prove a source of great weakness in case of disaster is the practical inconvertibility of the notes. True, the banks must maintain a redemption fund; but while this is a requirement onerous and expensive to the banks, it is not an absolute protection to the public, because this fund may consist wholly of greenbacks. Now, as a matter of fact, speaking financially, the National Bank notes are more valuable than the greenbacks, because the greenbacks are simply non-interest-bearing obligations of the government, while the National Bank notes are secured by the interest-bearing obligations of the same government, worth from ten to twenty-five per cent. more than the notes they secure, and this collateral is reinforced by a first lien on all the bank's assets and the liability of its stockholders to replace all impairments of the original capital.

It is manifest, therefore, that regarded simply as securities, the National Bank notes are of a higher order than the greenbacks, and hence the convertibility of the former into the latter is upon its face an inversion of terms.

The greenbacks, however, have an advantage over National Bank notes in two respects that may cause them to be preferred in certain contingencies; first, they are legal tender; second, they are redeemable in coin. Their legal-tender function, as we have seen, is an artificial force conferred by law, their convertibility into coin depends upon the ability of the government to maintain it upon a reserve of $100,000,000 of gold.

The total volume of National Bank currency outstanding November 1, 1892, as reported by the Comptroller of the Currency, page 4 of his Annual Report, was about $172,000,000. This was redeemable in greenbacks, and the greenbacks are by law redeemable in coin. To meet this obligation the Secretary of the Treasury holds $100,000,000 in gold against the total greenback issue of $346,000,000. Now in case a condition of things should arise leading to a run upon this reserve, holders of the National Bank notes would demand greenbacks for them and then use the greenbacks to obtain gold. Consequently the $100,000,000 of gold is the coin basis of the National Bank circulation and of the greenbacks also, which is $\frac{100}{518}$, or less than twenty per cent., of the circulation resting upon it, while under the old system the coin reserve was from thirty to forty per cent. From this point of view, therefore, the National Bank note circulation does not appear to be as well equipped, as to convertibility, as was the old State bank circulation.

This is not the place to discuss how the present system could be modified so as to preserve its advantages and remedy its defects, but enough has been said to suggest the direction in which improvements may be made with profit to the banks and convenience to the people. For the purpose of our present inquiry it is sufficient to show, as has been done in this chapter, that bank-notes may constitute a part of the general currency, and that there are many considerations of economy, convenience, and industrial advantage which favor their use under proper safeguards as to security and convertibility.

It being clear that, regarded merely as a substitute for coin, bank-notes are more profitable to a community than government notes, the next point is as to the relative liability to depreciation of these two kinds of currency. The first point of difference between them in this respect is fundamental, because it lies in the basis of their issue. As has been seen, the government notes are issued to creditors of the government, while the bank-notes are issued to debtors to the bank. The government "pays" its debts in its own notes, but the person so "paid" is really not paid until he has exchanged those notes for their face value in something else; all successive holders of the notes become in turn creditors of the government, which through its taxing power creates a debt to itself equal in amount to the aggregate of the debts it has put off by the device of "paying" them in its own notes, and also compels taxpayers to give their property for those notes in order to discharge their taxes by returning the notes to the Treasury.

A bank, on the other hand, issues its notes only to those who voluntarily become indebted to it, and the bank-notes are in effect the bank's endorsement or guarantee of that debt, on which the debtor is enabled to obtain, by means of the bank's credit, that which he could not get on his own credit, whether it be commodities, services, or gratifications.* The only way in which a bank of issue can put out circulation is by discounting paper, and in every case the maker of the paper becomes a debtor to the bank before he becomes its creditor by being a holder of its notes; in fact, he borrows the notes on his own credit or on that of his endorser, or on the validity of collateral security. Thus, for the redemption of its own notes the bank holds the security it exacts from its debtors, while against the government notes there is no provision for redemption but the government power to levy and to collect taxes.

It is true that when and as long as both the government notes and the bank-notes are convertible into coin on demand, they are mutually interconvertible, and therefore of equal value to the recipient; but since both are liable to become inconvertible into coin, it makes a great difference to the public whether the notes in their hands are tokens which are extinguished when used to discharge debts which the holders have voluntarily contracted with the banks, and of which they have already received the full worth, or are pledges of

* See Chapter XIII., page 145.

the government which, though legal tender for private debts, it can redeem only by exacting their surrender in satisfaction of taxes which its power enables it to levy, and which it is free to adjust to the outstanding volume of such pledges.

There is another point: No bank has any obligations inconsistent with that of preserving its solvency, so that every bank that is honestly and intelligently managed will generally have assets sufficient to meet its liabilities; but governments are subject to political and other influences tending to extravagance, and nothing is so well adapted for disguising extravagance as the power to issue paper money—nay, nothing is so conducive to extravagance as that, because, generally, currency inflation commands popular applause. On this ground, therefore, it is wiser to use banknotes than to permit the government to issue paper money. If among a multitude of banks a few become insolvent, the harm done is limited in scope, but when a government becomes extravagant, the mischief is wide-spread and incalculable.

CHAPTER XVI.

THE BALANCE OF TRADE

Every man in business understands what is meant by making his bank account good. He knows that however large may be the aggregate amount of his checks and deposits during the day, all that he has to be careful about is that the resulting balance is in his favor. If he begins the day with only one dollar in bank, he may draw checks for thousands, and even millions, and have them honored, provided he deposits cash, checks, or exchange, to an equal or greater amount, before the bank closes in the afternoon. The balance is the only thing regarded, either by the bank or by the merchant. If this is not settled the merchant is discredited, he is financially disabled.

When several banks are doing business in the same place, each will receive from its depositors checks upon the others. In settlements between these banks the balances only are regarded. If there is no clearing-house each bank pays to, or receives from, every other bank the balance resulting from mutual demands. If there is a clearing-house, each pays or receives its own general balance through that institution. Thus it appears that banks bring to a balance on their books the operations of their depositors and then settle balances between themselves, and that it is only these balances, and not the transactions from which they result, that are settled in money.*

Where there are banks and clearing-houses, therefore, all the varied operations of a great mercantile community may go on without any money passing, except what is required to settle balances, to pay wages, and to carry on the retail trade. The same principle obtains in settlements between cities. A bank in Chicago makes collections for, remits exchange to, and draws drafts upon, its correspondent bank in New York to a very large amount every day, but no money need be remitted, except to settle an adverse balance; nor can the New York bank be called upon to remit money to Chicago, unless the balance is in favor of the Chicago bank. The state of the balance between the two cities influences, but does not of itself alone determine, the rate of exchange on New York at Chicago; but the rate of exchange determines currency movements between the two

---

* As a matter of fact, some money is deposited in bank every day by people who have drawn no checks that day, or by those whose deposits exceed their drafts, and such money does not go into bank in order to settle balances, but such deposits are voluntary and for the convenience of the depositors; they are not made under stress of obligation, as are the deposits which make the bank account good.

cities, and practically brings it about that only the final balance between all the banks in Chicago, on the one hand, and their correspondents in New York, on the other, is settled in money.

The foreign trade of the country is carried on by means of bills of exchange payable in London, Paris, etc., the bankers here purchasing and remitting bills drawn against exports and supplying their own drafts to importers to pay for goods brought into the country. Here, again, it is the balance only that has to be settled in money. If the values imported exceed those exported, rates of exchange rise, and money must be shipped abroad; if exports exceed imports in value, exchange falls, and money comes from abroad.

It is interesting to observe that even amid the countless transactions of a great city, like New York or London, indeed in the vast volume of commerce between continents, the primary use and function of money still survive; values are exchanged (through checks and bills of exchange, mere counters) as they were in barter three thousand years ago; and the money comes in at the end only to "even the trade," to settle the balance. What is still more remarkable is that to-day such settlements between nations are made as Abraham settled with Ephron, by weighing the silver and gold; for whether coined or not, the precious metals in international trade pass by weight, *i.e.*, by intrinsic value, only; so difficult is it for man to escape the operations of natural laws.

Czars, Parliaments, and Congresses may coin metal and emit paper money, Latin unions, great nations, and many small communities may accept these and give them currency at arbitrary valuations, each within its own borders, but in the world's clearing-house world-wide values alone are available, and these must come in pure metal and must stand the test of accurate weighing. The natural law here seen in its primitive nakedness is present throughout society, only there it is clothed in conventional forms. A manufacturer may keep up a circulation of his own due-bills in the village clustered around his mill; but for raw material and supplies purchased outside he must pay the money current at the place of their purchase; hence he must exact this money in payment for his goods. Were it not for the Constitutional prohibition, a State might sustain among its citizens, by taxation, a currency of its own bills of credit, but beyond its borders they would be unavailable as money; so in the United States we use among ourselves greenbacks, National Bank notes, and standard silver dollars, but these will not pass at their home value in the settlement of balances in London, Paris, or Berlin.

Now the law of finance underlying all these instances is the law embodied in clearing-house rules, viz., that when several kinds of money are circulating in the community, all balances must be settled in that kind only which is available for the settlement of outside exchanges, and from this proposition there is deduced, as a corollary, the following principle, viz., that only what is available to settle balances at any money centre is good money throughout the entire area within which exchanges are focused on that centre.

The reason of this is obvious. A man who has to make good his balance in bank cannot accept from his debtor, or in payment for his services or wages, anything but what the bank will take, *i.e.*, what is known as bankable funds. The banks exact this because they, too, must meet all demands upon them, including their clearing-house balances, and they can do so only in such funds. The clearing-house cannot relax the rule, because if it did the community would, under the operation of Gresham's law, very soon lose all its wide-range money and have only a local circulation, unavailable for meeting the demands upon it from other places, and that unavailability would paralyze its business by embarrassing collections, thus discrediting its merchants and eventually crippling the banks themselves.

Now in determining what are bankable funds regard is had both to form and to definiteness of value. Requirement as to form is expressed in the term "cash," as ordinarily used, including money and "money-at-credit," * at the place of observation, while that as to definiteness of value is determined by the standard of money value (the monetary unit) at that financial centre which is the

* See Chapter II., page 16.

focus of exchange for the area in which the place of observation is situated. This being the case, it follows that no commercial community is entirely free to set up a local money of its own; if statute laws do not forbid, natural laws will hinder and embarrass the use of such money, while every commercial community finds its interest promoted by the largest possible local circulation of that currency, among all within its reach, which has the widest range.* In the United States no commercial city can afford to be without money that is good in New York. In New York and other financial centres there must always be a stock of money that is good in London. Even between 1862 and 1879 bankers and merchants engaged in the foreign trade at New York were compelled to keep a gold

---

* Different kinds of money are not always equally within reach of given communities. Of money as of everything else, the best goes to those who appreciate it most highly, and who can afford to own it. Some tribes are too poor to own a currency consisting wholly even of copper, others cannot afford much, if any, silver; vast populations in Asia and Africa are as yet unable to use gold to any extent, but manifestly each community should, and if not interfered with by governments would, hold of every kind of money the precise quantity indicated by its needs and its means. These quantities conform to the habits of the people. If in any given place the population consists of one-tenth who habitually carry more than $10 about them, one-tenth who carry between $5 and $10, three-tenths carrying between $1 and $5, and the remainder, who seldom have as much as a dollar at a time, nearly three-quarters of the whole number of coins in use must be under a dollar, and not more than one-tenth of the number can exceed $10. The amounts held depend upon other conditions not now to be considered.

currency circulating among themselves because that money alone would settle balances in Europe.

That was the only point east of the Rocky Mountains where such a currency was maintained, consequently by the end of this period the whole trade of the United States with Europe centred in New York more completely than ever before. It may be inferred that what was thus forced upon these bankers and merchants between 1862 and 1879 was a matter of immaterial consequence to the rest of the people of the United States; but this is not so. It costs a great deal to carry such a currency in that way, and the whole cost, besides a profit thereon and some compensation for the risk and trouble involved, were taken out of the proceeds of our exports and added to the cost of imports in the form of premiums of exchange. But this was not all the cost nor the greater part. During that period the premium on gold fluctuated between par and one hundred and eighty-five per cent., and as neither the producers of our exports nor the consumers of our imports could select the times at which exchange was to be sold against exports, or that at which bills must be bought to pay for imports, these two classes were at the mercy of dealers in exchange, and had to accept and pay currency prices, computed at extreme gold rates both ways. Consumers of protected articles suffered in the same way, because the premium on gold operated as an addition to the import duty.

Now, while the cost of carrying a metallic currency can never be wholly escaped, and while it is by no means inconsiderable, yet it is reduced to a minimum when that currency is circulating as money throughout the entire country, and besides, the cost then is so distributed as to be inappreciable at any one place or by any particular person or class. Both economy and mercantile convenience, therefore, indicate that each community should hold as part of its ordinary circulating medium whatever metallic money is needed as a reserve for the demands of its foreign trade.

Another consideration is important. Suppose having $600,000,000 in gold we have to export $10,000,000; that contracts the circulation $10,000,000. But if we held only $200,000,000 in gold, and it was all in the Treasury as a basis for a greenback or bank circulation of $600,000,000, then the export of $10,000,000 in gold would contract the circulation $30,000,000, because for every dollar withdrawn from the coin basis of such circulation, three dollars must be got out of circulation in one way or another, or else the proportion of reserve to outstanding notes is disturbed. For this reason, during the days of State banks of issue, every important demand for specie for export produced a spasm throughout the whole internal trade of the country, and if shipments continued, suspension and depreciation followed, because it was impossible to retire circulation with a celerity three or four times that of the gold movement. The book-credit system, to which the

English have been compelled to resort by the Procrustean Bank Act of 1844, is even more sensitive than our old State bank system used to be to gold exports and imports, and even until to-day the whole commercial and industrial machinery of Great Britain is accelerated or retarded by the influx or efflux of gold at the Bank of England.

There is no inconsistency between what is here said and what was said in the preceding chapter about the economy and efficiency of a bank-note circulation. The observations in the present chapter apply to a government currency like that of our greenbacks, the reserve for which is held wholly in the Treasury, whence it may be drawn in large blocks for export, and before 1862 the chief stock of gold was held in New York and at other seaports, where it was handy for export, whereas the preceding chapter describes a totally different state of things, such as would exist if the whole greenback circulation of \$346,000,000 were withdrawn and the banks were set free to supply paper money for the country, under proper regulation as to reserve and redemption. There are about six thousand of these institutions dispersed all over our territory, and if each of these were compelled to hold a specie reserve against its circulation, and a currency reserve, as now, against its deposits, the necessary stock of gold would be so distributed and so strongly held as to be practically beyond the reach of influences tending to its serious depletion by export.

CHAPTER XVII.

THE VOLUME OF MONEY

Much controversy exists as to what volume of money should be maintained in the United States, and conflicting theories on this subject compete for practical application through the coinage and currency laws. It is important for Congress to decide rightly among these theories, because, of course, there can be only one true theory, and if that one is not selected as the basis of legislation, harm rather than good will result. These theories have not been formulated with scientific precision: if they were, perhaps, some of them would not have so many adherents, but each has been tacitly accepted by some among those who favor the legislative measures which are the logical expression of the principles the theories severally set forth. The first, and apparently the most popular theory, is what may be called "the *per capita* requirement," which is, in effect, that the volume of money in the country should increase in some sort of proportion to the increase in the total number of inhabitants.

In considering this theory the first inquiry must be whether there is really, or can be, any relation between the number of people in the country and the number or the money amount of coins and notes existing at any particular time; because, of course, the whole theory of a *per capita* requirement of currency depends upon there being such a relation. If any argument exists in support of this postulate, I have not seen it. In the debates in Congress those who favored the silver legislation of the last twelve years used to cite certain figures as to the *per capita* supply of money in different countries as evidence that there should be more currency in the United States, and it may be that these figures are considered as supplying an argument of that character, but they do not even show any constant relation between currency and population anywhere; on the contrary, they indicate considerable diversity in this respect among the countries selected, and if we add the figures for Great Britain and Ireland, which ordinarily are omitted from the tables in the *Congressional Record,* we shall find the diversity still greater.

It seems useless to reproduce here the various tables referred to; some of them are now out of date, but the following table contains all the facts pertinent to the inquiry in hand. It has been compiled in the United States Mint Bureau, and includes the latest returns of population and circulation in the countries named:

MONETARY SYSTEMS AND APPROXIMATE STOCKS OF MONEY IN THE AGGREGATE AND PER CAPITA IN THE PRINCIPAL COUNTRIES OF THE WORLD.

Countries.	Monetary System.	Ratio between Silver. (Gold and Full Legal Tender)	Ratio between Gold and Limited Tender Silver.	Population.	Stock of Gold.	Stock of Silver. Full Tender.	Stock of Silver. Limited Tender.	Stock of Silver. Total.	Uncovered Paper.	Per Capita. Gold.	Per Capita. Silver.	Per Capita. Paper.	Per Capita. Total.
United States	Gold and Silver	1-15.98	1-14.95	65,000,000	$654,000,000	$498,000,000	$77,000,000	$575,000,000	$405,790,000	$10.06	$8.85	$6.24	$25.15
United Kingdom	Gold	1-15½	1-14.29	38,000,000	550,000,000		100,000,000	100,000,000	50,000,000	14.47	2.63	1.32	18.42
France	Gold and Silver	1-15.38	1-14.38	39,000,000	800,000,000	650,000,000	50,000,000	700,000,000	$1,402,000	20.52	17.95	2.09	40.56
Germany	Gold	1-13.957	49,500,000	600,000,000	103,000,000	108,000,000	211,000,000	107,000,000	12.12	4.26	2.16	18.54
Belgium	Gold and Silver	1-15½	1-14.38	6,100,000	63,000,000	48,400,000	6,600,000	55,000,000	54,000,000	10.66	9.02	8.85	28.53
Italy	Gold and Silver	1-15½	1-14.38	31,000,000	93,605,000	16,000,000	34,200,000	50,200,000	163,471,000	3.02	1.62	5.27	9.91
Switzerland	Gold and Silver	1-15½	1-14.38	3,000,000	15,000,000	11,400,000	3,600,000	15,000,000	14,000,000	5.00	5.00	4.67	14.67
Greece	Gold and Silver	1-15½	1-14.38	2,000,000	2,000,000		2,200,000	4,000,000	14,000,000	0.91	1.82	6.36	9.09
Spain	Gold and Silver	1-15½	1-14.38	18,000,000	40,000,000	120,000,000	38,000,000	158,000,000	100,000,000	2.22	8.78	5.56	16.56
Portugal	Gold		1-14.04	5,000,000	40,000,000			10,000,000	45,000,000	8.00	2.00	9.00	19.00
Austria-Hungary	Gold		1-13.69	40,000,000	40,000,000	90,000,000		90,000,000	260,000,000	1.00	2.25	6.50	9.75
Netherlands	Gold and Silver	1-15½	1-15	4,500,000	25,000,000	61,500,000	3,200,000	65,000,000	40,000,000	5.65	14.44	8.89	28.88
Scandinavian Union	Gold		1-14.88	8,600,000	32,000,000		10,000,000	10,000,000	27,000,000	3.72	1.16	3.14	8.02
Russia	Silver		1-15	113,000,000	250,000,000	22,000,000	38,000,000	60,000,000	500,000,000	2.21	0.53	4.42	7.16
Turkey	Gold and Silver	1-15½	1-15.1	33,000,000	50,000,000		45,000,000	45,000,000		1.52	1.36		2.88
Australia	Gold		1-14.28	4,000,000	100,000,000		7,000,000	7,000,000		25.00	1.75		96.75
Egypt	Gold		1-15.68	7,000,000	104,000,000		15,000,000	15,000,000		14.29	2.14		16.43
Mexico	Gold and Silver			11,600,000	5,000,000	50,000,000		50,000,000	2,000,000	0.43	4.31	0.17	4.91
Central America	Silver	1-16½		3,000,000		500,000		500,000	2,000,000		0.17	0.67	0.84
South America	Silver	1-15½		35,000,000	45,000,000	25,000,000		25,000,000	600,000,000	1.29	0.71	17.14	19.14
Japan	Gold and Silver	1-16.16		40,000,000	90,000,000	50,000,000		50,000,000	56,000,000	2.25	1.25	1.40	4.90
India	Silver	1-15		255,000,000		900,000,000		900,000,000	28,000,000		3.53	0.11	3.64
China	Silver			400,000,000		700,000,000		700,000,000			1.75		1.75
The Straits	Gold					100,000,000		100,000,000					
Canada	Gold	1-15½	1-14.95	4,500,000	16,000,000		6,000,000	5,000,000	40,000,000	3.56	1.11	8.89	13.66
Cuba, Haiti, etc	Gold			2,000,000	20,000,000	1,200,000	800,000	2,000,000	40,000,000	10.00	1.00	20.00	31.00
Total					3,632,605,000	3,449,100,000	553,500,000	4,002,700,000	2,629,663,000				

If, as appears from this table, no uniform proportion of currency to population exists as to countries, does any exist as to lesser communities, say our States, counties, cities, and towns, or the cities or provinces of the European countries referred to? Do we find anywhere the coins or the total currency in any community distributed among individuals equally or among households, according to the number of their respective members? The experience and the common-sense of every reader may be appealed to in derision of the notion that the number of people in a house, a town, a State, or the whole country, has anything to do with the total volume of the money held or required in each of these communities.

But if it were otherwise, if it could be shown, as it cannot be, that the industries of France, for example, are more prosperous than those of the United States because the French have more money *per capita* than we have, while those of Great Britain are less prosperous because there the *per capita* supply of currency is less than it is in the United States, it still would be necessary to the argument in favor of government issues here to prove that in France there is some power or authority superior to our government in financial sagacity which has provided such a supply of currency, an assumption fatal to the agitation for government action here, because neither in France nor in any other country having more currency *per capita* than we have, has any government at any time undertaken to regulate the supply of money; while in every European country in which the *per capita* circulation exceeds that of the United States the present tendency is toward reduced supply through the suspension of silver coinage. The disparity shown in the tables simply proves that everywhere but here governments accept the doctrine which requires them to refrain from meddling in commercial adjustments, and especially to refrain from any attempt to increase or diminish the volume of money by administrative measures or by legislative enactment.

Another theory is, that the volume of currency should increase with increased wealth, and while no statistics have been adduced, this seems a reasonable conjecture if hazarded as to what is likely to happen under conditions unfettered by legislation and undisturbed by government interference. This is indeed the true doctrine on this subject, as may easily be substantiated without going abroad, by examining those facts which are familiar to all, however meagre may have been their experience.

The trouble with most writers and statesmen is, that they look at these matters wholly in a general far-off way and take no note of what passes daily before their eyes. Now the facts connected with currency distribution and movements over great areas and among large populations are difficult of discovery and impossible of precise ascertainment, because of the incessant mobility of money; while on the other hand, facts as to the normal movement of coins and notes in any particular locality are readily obtainable, and these facts are not only sufficient for our purpose, but they are the only facts that can be relied upon, both as to authenticity and pertinence. These facts establish the principle that the office and function of money is to pass from hand to hand, and a corollary deduced therefrom is that, except while actually so passing, coins and notes are, as far as their effect goes, not money at all; they are equivalent to bullion, unsigned bank or Treasury notes, or anything else convertible into money without change of substance.

Whatever money, therefore, is hoarded, whatever is held up in banks, whatever is otherwise out of circulation, constitutes reserve of material available for circulation, but it is not a part of the active circulation, hence the tables above referred to are misleading, because in interpreting them it is generally assumed that all the money in each country is in circulation, whereas it is never all in circulation, and no one knows how much of it is circulating at any particular time of day or night.

In order to examine the subject somewhat definitely, let us define active circulation as money that changes hands at least once a day. The moment we get down to this plane of practical observation, we remember that a great deal of money is constantly lying unhandled, while also we think of cases where the same money changes hands many times a day, and it at once becomes manifest that what is unused should not count, and that the effective force of what is used is greatly increased by repetition of employment. One dollar that changes hands ten times a day does the duty of ten dollars in liquidating debt, effecting exchanges, and measuring values, which are the only uses of dollars as money; but the dollars resting in some man's pocket, or till, or safe, are functionless.*

Now any theory of money distribution or currency supply must be defective that does not take account of the increased effectiveness of money, by reason of repetition of employment, and also of the proportion between active circulation and reserve which obtains in different communities. These two principles are really what control the quantity of money required in any community, at any given time, and because these vary incessantly and independently, while the population is nearly constant numerically, it is impossible for the *per capita* requirement theory to have any

---

* These dollars are property; they have value; the time will come when they will resume activity, but meanwhile, as long as they rest in pocket, till, or vault they are unprofitable property, yielding no revenue performing no service; nor is money thus idle merely unprofitable, it is an expense, and at the great financial centres, where money is handled in blocks large enough to make the expense appreciable, it is lent from day to day at merely nominal rates, so as to mitigate this expense. Each man tries to shift upon another the burden of idle money, each bank, each community, each country makes the same effort.

foundation in reason, or to find any support from facts.

Legislation, therefore, influenced in any degree by efforts to apply this theory, is misguided and likely to prove injurious. To illustrate this view of the subject, money may be compared to the rolling-stock of a railroad. Money is an instrument of exchange through the transportation of value; railroad cars are instruments of exchange through the transportation of commodities; both classes of instruments are useful only when performing their respective functions; at other times, without losing value, they are an encumbrance and an expense. The number of dollars or vehicles at any time in use depends upon the volume of business to be accommodated; a railroad subject to extreme variations in the volume of traffic must either maintain during dull periods a considerable number of idle cars and locomotives, or else in times of activity it must be able to hire what it lacks; so merchants and communities subject to variations in the volume of their business must either keep idle money of their own during the dull periods, or they must hire enough to supply their needs during periods of activity.

A railroad that has the same amount and kind of traffic both ways every day, all the year round, works at the minimum of expense in rolling-stock, because it is able to adjust the number of locomotives and cars to its needs, and to get the maximum of work out of every locomotive and car it owns by keeping them all incessantly going, while another road, of the same length, may be at much greater expense, because it has all its heavy traffic one way, and occurring in spurts at irregular intervals. Now what railroad manager would disregard these considerations and fix the number and capacity of the locomotives and cars for each road by the length of its track, or in proportion to the population of the country through which it runs?

In the same way one community using about the same amount of currency every day needs to keep on hand only that precise amount, because every coin and note is in constant use, while in another community of the same size opposite conditions may prevail. What, then, becomes of the principle of *per capita* distribution? Manifestly the best thing for railroads generally is that each company should be free and able to adjust the number of its locomotives and cars to its average needs, to hire out its idle stock when its own traffic is dull, to hire from its neighbors in times of activity. Now upon reflection it will appear that four things are necessary in order that a railroad should be able to conduct its business in that way; these are:

1st. That there are other railroads near by managed on the same principle.

2d. That the number and mutual independence of these should be sufficient to afford a guarantee against combinations to make a "corner" in rolling-stock at a critical moment.

3d. That the group of railroads thus interchanging should be so circumstanced as to render it more or less certain that no excessive proportion of them will reach their periods of maximum need simultaneously.

This requirement will be more or less fully complied with in proportion as the area covered by the interchanging roads is extended, and also in proportion as the nature of their traffic is diversified.

4th. That these roads should have their tracks of the same gauge and connecting, their locomotives adapted to the same fuel, their couplings interacting, and all other physical conditions adjusted to the free use of any vehicle on every road.

The manifest advantages attending such arrangements have contributed to the consolidation of distinct railroads into great systems, to the union of these systems in associations, and, a few years ago, to the change of gauge over a large section of country. As a further step in the application of this principle companies have been formed expressly to build cars and hire them out.*

Now within fifty years our railroads have marvellously increased in number and extension; this whole system of car-interchanging has come into

* The relation of these companies toward the railroads is the same as that of banks and other lenders of money toward merchants and others who have to use money, while the relation of different railroads to each other as hirers of cars is like the relation between different communities under which money is transferred from one to another through operations in exchange.

existence and attained proportions but little appreciated by the general public, and although producers and consumers of every sort and everywhere are vitally dependent upon the uninterrupted use of the facilities of transportation they afford, there is among the people absolute confidence that the managers of these roads can and will provide cars and locomotives enough for all purposes. No one has dreamed of suggesting that the supply of these should be proportioned to the population; no one has proposed that the government should build locomotives and cars, as it was for years coining silver dollars and is now issuing coin notes against silver bullion, or that, having built them, it should store them up in order that the railroads may be sure of having an adequate supply.

If such measures were adopted they would immediately disturb railroad management throughout the United States; every workshop for the manufacture of locomotives and cars would curtail its operations, stop the purchase of raw material, of castings, fittings, etc.; the purveyors of these articles would find their business paralyzed, and, after fifteen years of government effort to increase the supply of rolling-stock, there would be fewer locomotives and cars in the country than if the railroads had been left alone. All the sources and channels of supply of the raw materials and fittings, except those favored by the government, would be dried up; all other workshops would be idle, the skilled hands unemployed, the capital invested in buildings and machinery lost.

Is this not a striking likeness of the consequences of the effort made by the government to increase the supply of money in the country by first coining two million dollars' worth of silver every month and afterward buying, with notes issued for the purpose, 4,500,000 ounces of silver monthly? Are not the banks surrendering their circulation; are not credits curtailed; have not gold coins, estimated to amount to $600,000,000, disappeared entirely from ordinary circulation; have not greenbacks become rare? Who ever sees or handles any money now except silver coins, silver certificates, or coin notes? Statesmen tell us we require vastly more than $1,800,000,000 of currency; the Bland Law, which was designed to increase the volume of currency in circulation, has contracted it to half that sum, and the passage of the law of July, 1890, increasing the purchases of silver to 4,500,000 ounces per month, was followed immediately by monetary stringency.

But it is not only in the passage of these laws that the quantity theory of money has found expression in our national legislation. Nearly all the laws relating to the currency, and to the fiscal operations of the government, passed within the last twenty years, have been more or less shaped by the theory that in one way or another the welfare of the people could be promoted by an increase in the volume of that part of the circulating medium which owes its existence to governmental creation. That this is a fallacy will clearly appear upon application to money of the principles obviously governing the supposed case of Congress undertaking to promote the welfare of the people interested in transportation by the governmental manufacture of freight cars.

To estimate the full effect of such legislation let us suppose that Congress, in undertaking to build some theoretical number of freight cars every month, should also enact a law that the railroads should charge freight by the car-load and not by the ton, and then should order the government cars built to carry just twenty tons, because the cars of thirty years ago were of that capacity, or because India, Mexico, and certain other countries are satisfied with such cars.* At first, of course, all the railroads having bigger cars and powerful locomotives, heavy rails, ballasted road-bed, and other arrangements and equipments to correspond, would protest; but in fifteen years the government cars would have supplanted the others, the heavy rails would have been replaced with lighter ones, the expense of keeping up the road-bed would have been saved, and the people would have been

---

* There would be just as much reason for this as for insisting that in 1893 412½ grains of 90 fine silver should carry a full dollar because it did so in 1876, or because France first, and the Latin Union afterward, held silver at a stable value among their own people for seventy years, or because the Mexican dollar and the Indian rupee have been unchanged in weight notwithstanding their decline in value.

gradually and imperceptibly forced up to paying as much for moving twenty tons as they used to pay for moving forty, and our railroad system would be back to where it was thirty years ago; the people poorer, and the owners of railroad stock richer.

This is what has happened after fifteen years of the Bland Law and its successor, the Silver Act of 1890. At first the bankers and capitalists, having all their arrangements adjusted to a currency resting on gold and amounting to $1,800,000,000, protested against the law; but now they have adapted their arrangements to that law, and they are contentedly absorbing the profits of the present and looking forward with resignation to the still greater profits that will be forced upon them when the currency drops to the bullion value of the silver dollar. But, since reasoning by analogy is not always conclusive, it may be well to look upon this question from another point of view.

Ordinarily when a man receives money he puts in bank or lays away at home what he expects to spend, and invests the rest as profitably as he can; another who finds himself for the moment without the precise money needed for a special purpose, borrows on the best terms he can, or else he sells some kind of property, or, lastly, he gives up the contemplated transaction. Now since communities, however populous or geographically extended, consist wholly of individuals, and since all individuals are governed, in respect to these matters, by the same impulses and considerations, it follows that the supply of currency in every community will be distributed at any particular moment according, first, to the relative desire of different individuals to use particular amounts, immediately or prospectively; and, secondly, according to the relative ability of these individuals to obtain the amounts they severally desire.

The amount desired by each man is divisible into what he desires for immediate use, and what he thinks it expedient to keep in hand for his future needs. Now in every widely extended community of diversified and active industry the amount of currency passing from hand to hand, day by day, under ordinary conditions of business and confidence, will be about the same at all times, but the amount held up by each individual to meet future requirements will vary greatly from time to time.

If anything causes a large proportion of the individuals in any community to simultaneously accumulate currency, each having regard only to his own requirements, immediate and future, the aggregate of such withdrawals from the volume of currency will reduce that portion available for active circulation below the current needs in the community, and produce what is commonly called "a scarcity of money." It is a natural law, resulting from the uniformity of human action under like conditions, that a general opinion that such a scarcity is likely to arise tends of itself to produce that scarcity, because every man in endeavoring to provide himself with money enough to tide over the apprehended "squeeze," holds up all the money he can, and so helps to precipitate that very condition against which he is endeavoring to guard.

Now in spite of whatever efforts governments may make, no community ever retains for any length of time a greater volume of circulation than will suffice for its ordinary needs; as has been already said, idle money is an encumbrance and an expense, like idle railroad cars, and the uniformity of human action under like conditions leads each man, each bank, each city, each country, to shift upon some other the burden of superfluous currency. Hence through the export of coin, or the curtailment of credits, or the diminished use of checks, drafts, and notes (which ordinarily constitute the largest part of the active currency of industrial communities), the total volume of circulation in each community will become adjusted to the normal volume of its business, or else the volume of money being beyond control, an equilibrium will be reached by the expanse of *speculation* and an inflation in the prices of speculative investments.*

There is, therefore, always a tendency, under normal conditions of business and of political and

---

* It is undeniable that only speculative investments are raised in price by temporary money surfeits, but the reaction invariably depresses real estate and commercial values, while the curtailment of credit incident to periods of inflation becomes aggravated when the fever of speculation subsides.

social tranquillity, toward the establishment of an equilibrium between the average volume of daily cash transactions and the volume of the circulation, including in this term the checks, drafts, notes, and credits which take the place of "lawful" money. This being the case, when an occasion arises, as above described, impelling a general resort to the holding up of money, scarcity is inevitable, and as such scarcity always breeds distrust and renders instruments of credit for the time being more or less unavailable as substitutes for money, the exclusion of these from their customary office aggravates the effects of the currency contraction.

It is evident, therefore, that no amount of money emitted by the government can avert periods of scarcity, and there are those who think that the somewhat regular recurrence of such periods is inevitable. It is, however, equally evident that the greater the area covered by any single monetary system, the greater the number of persons participating in the custody and daily handling of the circulating medium, the more diversified the situation, occupation, interest, thoughts, and feelings of these individuals, the less likelihood will there be of any occurrence producing a unanimous and simultaneous movement toward the holding up of money.

At the same time, if all over this area, through the agency of banks and the other appliances of modern finance, a free movement of money is practicable, from one individual or bank or town or city or country to another, a temporary increase of need at one point will generally be coincident with a temporary superfluity at another, and the community as a whole would keep as part of its normal volume of currency whatever amount might be required to be passed around in this way to meet successive temporary demands at different localities. In this way actual scarcity would be prevented to a great extent, and the effect of an apprehension of scarcity would be reduced to the minimum.

It follows that periods of stringency are less likely to occur in proportion as the area and population under one monetary system become enlarged, and hence it may be inferred that if the whole world were under a uniform monetary system, such occurrences would be reduced to the minimum, if they were not rendered impossible.

It is plain, from this view of the subject, that while the welfare of the people of any given country can never be promoted by excessive emissions of money by the government, it may be very greatly promoted by their being brought into such association with the people of other countries that a uniform monetary system may prevail over as great an area as possible, their own territory forming a part of it. If there is any advantage, as the Fathers of our Republic believed, in securing to all the people of the United States a general uniform monetary system, instead of leaving them as they had been during the colonial period, and as they were under the Confederation, subject to systems limited by State boundaries; if we should find it intolerable now to go back to the condition from which our predecessors were rescued by the Constitution, or even to that prevailing up to 1862, then manifestly our welfare would be still more promoted, our monetary condition would be still more assured, if our sixty-two millions of people could be brought into union with the people of all other countries that have attained to our plane of industrial development, and if these united hundreds of millions, distributed as they are so widely over the globe, could all come under one uniform monetary system.

The great majority of people are led to favor the *per capita* theory of money, not because they believe in it as a theory, but because it affords ground for increased issues of money by the government, and they think that such increased issues will promote prosperity by "making money plentiful."

Let us therefore examine this latter proposition.

It will require few words to prove that the mere plentifulness of money in any given place can in no way benefit any person. Thousands of people who live and labor in rural communities, where money is perennially scarce, are better off than they possibly could be if they should be suddenly removed to New York, where, comparatively speaking, money is always plentiful. Again, take two banks, side by side in New York, one a large bank with millions of money in its vaults and another a small bank with only thousands under its roof. The clerks and the porters and the messengers of one are no better off than those of the other; comparing them, man with man, and service with service, certainly the hucksters at the doors are not affected by the wealth within, nor are the customers better served by the big bank than by the small one; generally it is the other way.

If one tries to think out the details of any conceivable process by which the mere plentifulness of money benefits any individual, he will find that he has to suppose certain conditions of means, opportunities, abilities, and purposes, all of which must be combined before such an individual can appropriate any advantage to himself from the plentifulness of money, and then upon a close analysis it will be found that the advantage arises out of that combination, and not out of the plentifulness of money. It is true that plentifulness of money excites speculation, but speculation diverts both men and capital from productive industrial employment, which is a loss of wealth-producing force, and in all speculation some lose what others gain, while both parties suffer in moral tone. In this respect, therefore, plentifulness of money is an evil, not a blessing.

The fundamental fallacy of this whole notion,

that the government should make money plentiful, lurks probably in a confusion of ideas about the effect of an abundant supply of money. We are all accustomed to connect abundance of supply with cheapness, and in one sense this connection applies to money, but not in the sense that is generally assumed. Money is the only thing of which the dearness or cheapness is estimated by its rental value expressed in a percentage of itself. Money is said to be dear or cheap according to the rate of interest demanded for its use; while lands, houses, corn, or cotton are called dear or cheap according to the amount of money paid for the transfer of their ownership from a seller to a buyer.

Bearing in mind this distinction, it is easily seen that the dearness or cheapness of money must depend primarily upon the relation between the supply of loanable funds and the demand for the use of such funds, and it will also appear that the total amount of currency existing in any particular country can only remotely affect the incessant variations of this relation at numerous points all over the country. The term, loanable funds, is by no means restricted to actual money. Nearly all loans are made by credits entered on the books of a bank, or by checks or drafts or acceptances, and these pass into the general clearings of the community, of which only the resulting balances are settled in money, hence the mere plentifulness of money is only remotely connected with the supply of loanable funds. The state of trade, the prosperity of the community, the degree of confidence in the immediate future, and the general state of credit, immediately and directly, influence both lending and borrowing. Whatever tends to depress these, tends to raise the price of money by decreasing the supply of loans and increasing the demand for them, and *vice versa*, whatever tends to improve trade and augment prosperity, whatever increases general confidence and strengthens credit, tends to make money cheaper by encouraging lenders and rendering borrowers less eager.

Now unnecessary, unwise, or ill-considered augmentations in the volume of the currency tend to produce the conditions that inevitably make money scarce and raise the rate of interest; because—

1st. They tend to unsettle values, and in that way to disturb trade adjustments, which disturbance in turn impairs confidence and abridges credit. Consequently lenders of money become timid and borrowers become more eager, money is held out of circulation and people say it is scarce.

2d. They tend to excite speculation, and that draws capital away from employment in productive industries in order that it may be used (as it always can be more profitably) in speculative operations. The capital thus withdrawn, is, of course, that which has been heretofore borrowed by the industrial producer, hence he must borrow anew and at a higher rate, or else curtail his operations. This influence soon makes itself felt throughout the whole sphere of industrial production, because such production is carried on largely by means of borrowed capital, and its general effect is manifested in higher interest, reduced wages, smaller profits, diminished production and dearer goods.

3d. A government that assumes to itself the function of continually increasing the volume of money never reaches a point at which it can stop, because each augmentation tends to make money dearer, and since the object is to make money cheaper, there will always be a clamor to increase the scale of annual augmentations. A government so situated is like a horse going down hill in a wagon without brakes: he must ever be going faster and faster, and yet at each stride he augments the momentum of the mass that is pushing him to destruction.

While it is the office and the duty of governments to so provide by law that the people's money may be the best possible, it must be remembered that the government does not give money away to individuals, or distribute it throughout the community; its whole duty is to determine what shall be money in order that those who can find a market for their labor, or products, or property, may be assured of receiving truly the value they bargain for. The demand for these determines their value and exchangeability, irrespective of the supply of money in the Treasury, in the banks, or in the community at large. No man can get money until he finds a buyer for what he has to sell, and buyers are not simply those who have money, but those who, having money or credit, have also the need or desire to possess the particular things one has to sell and who are able or willing to pay the price asked.

Simply making money plentiful, therefore, cannot exercise the least influence to increase the demand for any man's labor or products. A tradesman may have millionaires passing his shop every day without selling them anything, while he drives a good trade with boot-blacks and others whose means are limited and precarious, but who desire the goods he deals in, while the millionaire does not want them. If the money in the pockets of the passer-by brings no increase of trade to a shop, how can such increase come to it because of money lying in bank or held in the national Treasury?

It follows from this that it is no part of the duty of the government, in providing money for its people, to attempt to create supplies of money to any amount, arbitrarily or hypothetically determined upon in advance. The laws can and should be so framed as that the quantity of money in circulation will be determined, from day to day, by the demand for it. It is the demand for money, the extent of the need for its use, that should regulate its quantity; this demand cannot be stimulated, this need cannot be extended by arbitrarily increasing the quantity of money in the country. A gas company cannot increase the demand for light by increasing the daily products of its works: it may dishonestly increase the consumption by maintaining an unnecessary pressure—that is all; but such conduct inflicts loss upon its customers, and in like manner a government which, by the operation of its laws, or the administration of its Treasury, creates an artificial pressure of unemployed money, injures its people, the users of its money, just as the users of gas are injured by an excessive pressure in the mains.

Since money performs its functions as a medium of exchange by passing from hand to hand, its effectiveness depends upon the number of exchanges effected by the same money in a given time. Rapidity and smoothness of circulation, not greatness of volume, give effectiveness to a currency; for the incessant variations in the activity of trade are perfectly and naturally accommodated by corresponding self-adjusted and delicately modulated variations in the rate of circulation, while variations in the volume of money disturb and obstruct trade, because they not only alternately impede and accelerate the circulation, but they do so artificially and violently. To attempt to stimulate trade and so to increase general prosperity by creating a volume of money greater than can be used effectively, is not only futile but pernicious, because it inflicts, either upon the government or the people, the expense of carrying so much dead capital.*

* This reasoning is sustained by a striking historical instance. Spain and Portugal acquired the richest mines of gold and silver in the world, and established colonies in those parts of America having the greatest natural advantages, as evidenced by the fact that there the aboriginal races had attained to the greatest degree of wealth. Up to that time both Spain and Portugal had been great commercial nations, and Spain had been powerful in a military and naval way. These countries drew all the silver and gold they could from their colonies, coined it into money, and then kept it, or tried to keep it, all within their own territories, by at one time prohibiting its export under severe penalties, and at another laying a heavy export duty upon it.

In consequence of thus gorging themselves with money, even though it was all pure silver and gold, and got out of the Mexicans and Peruvians without giving an equivalent, both these two countries began at once to decline in commercial importance as well as in military power, manufactures, and agriculture, while even in civilization they have lagged behind the age.

This consequence need not seem surprising when it is remembered that every dollar in money is a dollar idle; that every man who gives labor, or land, or machinery, or good security that bears interest, in exchange for money, and keeps that money, has exchanged productive capital for dead capital.

The Government of Spain in forcing its people to keep the immense value of their gold and silver in money instead of leaving them free to trade that money off for productive investments, burdened them with just so much dead capital, which cost, to carry it, all that the productive capital of the country could earn.

CHAPTER XVIII.

VALUE

Up to this point we have busied ourselves entirely with money as a fact, tracing its origin, its development, and its functions, as they are revealed by history and observation, and examining its basis in natural law, in industry, and in statute law. We have seen that every form of money depends for its circulation upon public confidence, and for its effectiveness upon the definiteness and stability of its value. It has been shown that wherever several kinds of money are to circulate indiscriminately, they must be co-ordinated and unified in function by being predicated upon a single monetary unit, and that there is no other way of effecting this result.

The material and forms of money, and the various substitutes for money were next investigated; the subject of legal tender was treated; the principles of a due-bill circulation were examined and applied; the term "balance of trade" was explained; and, finally, an inquiry was made as to the principles governing variations in the volume of circulation. So far, therefore, we have been dealing with concrete matters only; now it is necessary to take up the subject of value. Value is an abstract term expressing a relation. It is not a thing perceptible by the senses; indeed, it does not exist at all in the objects said to possess it, but is imputed to them by human intelligence. Value, therefore, is not a quality of objects, but only an attribute with which they become invested.

Value is very different from utility, though utility is generally, but not always, the basis of value. In ordinary speech the two words are often used indiscriminately, which is a constant source of confusion of ideas as to the true nature of value. Utility is a physical relation, whereas value is an abstract relation. Brute animals have a perception of utility; they have no conception of value. There are utilities in the animal and vegetable kingdoms that exist independently of mankind; but value is a purely human conception. Value may be primarily and generically defined as the relation between human desire and proximate objects of human pursuit. Those things with which nature supplies us gratuitously are not objects of pursuit, and therefore they are not invested with value; those things which being desired can be attained only by exertion, by sacrifice, or in exchange for things already belonging to us are invested with value.

It is obvious, therefore, that it cannot be any special quality in the thing desired which gives value to it, but that the value comes wholly from unsatisfied desire. It is true this desire is excited by our knowledge of the qualities of the thing, and by our opinion that those qualities render the thing desirable; but this knowledge and this opinion are in our minds, they are not in the thing, and it is in our minds that they excite the desire to possess the thing; they render it an object of pursuit, and establish between it and the desire that craves it that relation which we call value. Value being a relation, it must vary by degrees, not by quantities; and degrees of value, since value is the correlative of desire, must vary with the intensity of the desires to which they are related. But since value attaches only to that which, though desired, is as yet withheld from our possession, then value must vary also with the resistance to appropriation.

We have now two opposite influences simultaneously operating to control the variations of value: one in the man, viz., the intensity of his desire to possess a certain thing; the other in his environment, viz., the obstacles to his attainment of the object of that desire. Let us see whether these influences can be measured and compared. Suppose a man desires several things, and is uncertain which one of them he desires most. If he is a civilized man, he quickly solves the problem by considering which he is willing to give the most money for; if he is an uncivilized man, he also soon determines which he is willing to make the most exertion to obtain. We may, therefore, measure the intensity of such desires by money or else by human exertion, say by hours or days of labor or of pursuit. On the other hand, the same modes of measurement are applicable to the resistance to be overcome in obtaining possession of different objects of pursuit; under civilization, cost, outside of civilization, intensity and duration of exertion, measure the obstacles to appropriating any desired object. Value, therefore, is measured by money or by human exertion during certain intervals of time. Whatever men will pay for, work for, or fight for, is a thing possessing the attribute of value, and the degree of value in each case is determined wholly by the amount of money or of effort that the thing will command, and not at all by the nature of the thing itself. But, it will be said, things already possessed have value. This is true, for their possession by one man is an obstacle to their appropriation by others; but it is only the desire of others to appropriate them that gives them value when in the hands of their possessor. In this reasoning care must be taken not to confuse value with utility, and also to distinguish between actual and potential value. A thing may be indispensably useful to me; but if nobody else is ever likely to want it, it is destitute of value.* If, under certain possible contingencies, others may come to desire it, then it has *potential* value.

* A false tooth, a glass eye, a glove contrived to disguise the mutilation or deformity of the hand, are illustrations of useful objects that have no value when once possessed.

Let us illustrate this. A and B wear glasses of the same grade, and are dependent upon them. In company with a number of persons not needing glasses they go out for several days' excursion on the plains. There they meet a pedler who has for sale one pair of spectacles of the grade they use. A and B having glasses already, and the rest of the party not needing them at all, the pedler's spectacles have no actual value, *i.e.*, no value at that time and place. The pedler, however, knows that sooner or later he will meet some one who does want these spectacles, and, therefore, they have to him potential value. But A and B are both upset out of the wagon at the same time, and their glasses are smashed. Suddenly the pedler's single pair of spectacles acquire actual value, not through any change in them, but in consequence of the desire of A and B to possess them. Their utility is precisely what it was before, but owing to circumstances they have passed from the condition of valuelessness to that of value in the estimation of A and B, while in the estimation of the pedler they have passed from the condition of potential to that of actual value, and the degree of their value has been greatly enhanced. If A alone or B alone wanted the spectacles, or if only one of the two could afford to buy them, their value would be the point of practical adjustment between the intensity of desire for them on the part of that one and the intensity of the pedler's desire to make a large profit; but when both A and B compete for the spectacles, the original obstacle to their appropriation by either, viz., the pedler's estimate of their potential value, becomes increased by the intensity of the desire for them by the other. Supposing the pedler to offer the spectacles at auction, their value would then be determined by the willingness or the ability of one or the other of these two competitors to outbid the other.

This illustration is drawn from an exceptional case, but it is necessary in all analyses to eliminate conditions foreign to the precise matter to be determined in order to obtain definite and positive results. Here the transaction has been insulated so as to show that value is not a quality, but an attribute as respects the thing said to possess value, and that it is also a relation between that thing and the desire of one or more persons either to retain or to acquire it. Beyond this, the object is to show that as an attribute only, value is potential, indefinite, undetermined, conditional, and that it only becomes actual, definite, and determined when it is conditioned, and has assumed the aspect of a relation between the thing desired and one or more persons desiring it.

A relation between terms constant in respect to their nature, can vary only in degrees corresponding with the possible degrees of variations in the quality or force (*i.e.*, the "quantity") of either or both of such terms. The force of gravitation produces relations somewhat like those expressed by the term "value." We are accustomed to speak of the weight of bodies as we speak of the value of commodities, but weight is not a quality of such bodies; it is merely an attribute expressive of a relation between the earth's mass and any other mass suspended ponderably within reach of the earth's attraction. The terms of this relation are the earth, and any one or more ponderable bodies, and the relation between them varies in degrees corresponding with the mass and density of either term modified by their distance apart; hence differences in weight are measured in degrees. In most instances where gravity comes into play, the earth's attraction is regarded as a constant quantity; hence the general rule is to consider the degrees of this attraction as varying with the mass and density of particular bodies; but the variations of the barometer at different altitudes, the variations of tides consequent upon a modification of the earth's attraction by that of the sun and the moon, are familiar instances of a variation of weight arising out of a variation of the earth's spacial relation to the body, the mass and density of the body being constant.

Now, ordinarily, value varies according to demand and supply, as the phrase goes, and ordinarily demand is assumed to be as constant as the earth's mass is, while supply, being visibly variable, is represented by the mass and density of the lesser body. If, in the illustration employed above, the pedler had had two pairs of spectacles, the demand and supply would have stood at their normal equation, the spectacles would have shown their true weight in value, so to speak; but whenever and wherever there are two or more buyers to only one commodity, there is a monopoly, which produces a disturbance of the normal equation of value as determined by the world's demand and supply. If there had been two pedlers, each with a pair of spectacles for sale, with no occasion for combination, and A and B had dealt with them separately, this normal condition of things would have been maintained, and the spectacles could have been bought at what is called a fair price, viz., cost to the seller, with a reasonable and just profit added.

Now, let us go back to physical relations for further analogies. While all matter is subject to the force of gravity, and under ordinary conditions that is a constant force, certain substances are subject to other forces which, because they tend to modify the influence of gravity, are habitually measured by the degrees in which they effect such modification. Motion is one of these forces; magnetism is another. Motion, like weight, is not a quality; neither, however, is it an attribute, as weight and value are. It is simply a condition or state of being expressive of a series of progressive relations between the object in motion and definite points in time and space. Magnetism, finally (as far as science yet knows), is simply a relation— a relation to which such forms of value as that attributed to precious stones and objects of art come nearer in analogy than anything else in the world of physics.

These analogies may help us to understand how value, in its generic sense, covers several kinds of relations, for it may be the product of one or more of several forces, corresponding severally with the force of gravity, the force of motion and the force of magnetism. As weight is the relation between the earth's mass and any body suspended ponderably within the scope of the earth's attraction, so value, in a general sense, is the relation between the world's demand and any commodity suspended commercially within the scope of the world's attainment. Again, as motion is a relation between, on the one hand, the body moving, and, on the other hand, definite points in time and space, so "value in exchange" (money or its equivalents) is the relation between the commodities serving as money, on the one hand, and definite standards or fixed points of value, on the other. Finally, as magnetism is a simple relation of elective affinity, so the intrinsic value of precious stones and objects of art seems to express that intensity of desire which distinguishes the pursuit of gratifications from the pursuit of objects of mere utility.*

* To illustrate this characteristic of human nature, it is necessary only to observe how men risk their lives for honor or for gain, how they squander health and wealth in passionate excesses; how, finally, while believing the doctrine of eternal damnation, they consciously devote their souls forever to the fires of Hell, for the sake of slaking, for a moment, a thirst for sensual gratification.

If the doctrine of value as here laid down is now clearly apprehended, we may proceed to apply it to the subject of money. Money has been defined as value in exchange; its physical analogue is matter in motion. Now, motion is a force, as gravity is; but motion is a dynamic force; gravity is a static force. If we conceive of value as a relation produced by forces in action, we see its source in, first, the forces which impel men to the pursuit of objects to which they attribute value, and secondly, those which lead them to hold possession of valuable things already acquired; and regarding the first as dynamic, and the second as static, we may express the preponderance of the one or the other in any relation by the same terms, *i.e.*, we may distinguish between static value and dynamic value, meaning respectively value at rest and value in action. In the light of this conception, it may clarify our views of money to regard it as a value in action. It does exhibit some of the characteristics of force. It is a debt-paying force under statute law; a labor-compelling force, and a purchasing force under industrial laws. Now, forces to be utilized must be measured, and their measurement is expressed in degrees of force, while the mode or scale of measurement depends upon a fixed standard. As far as this analogy can lead to any conclusion (but of course there is no such thing as demonstration by analogy), the conclusion to which it leads is that established by previous reasoning, viz., that money to be useful, even as a debt-paying force, must be permanently related to some fixed standard of value.

There is, however, an application of the doctrine of value, which just at the point now reached in our inquiry is more important than the conception of it as a relation between forces. Commerce deals in commodities; finance deals in values. Commodities are things classified according to their substance, their utility and their distribution; values are things classified according to their value, without regard to substance, utility, or distribution. Commerce seeks to satisfy demand by means of supply, but its sole method is the interchange of commodities—it can have no other method. Finance facilitates commerce by adjusting inequalities of value arising out of such interchanges; it supplies to modern trade the same adjunct that money supplied to primitive barter; it settles balances, as money originally supplied the "boot,"—"evened the trade."

Regarded as a whole, commerce is really reducible to a complicated system of barter, of which finance is employed in keeping an account. The commodities exchanged in bulk by commerce are here measured by value, regardless of their substance. Every invoice is represented by a bill of lading describing its substance (commercial force) and a bill of exchange specifying its value (financial force). Bankers deal in these, and when balances arise between individuals, cities, sections, or countries, bankers (who are merchants of money) transfer the " boot " that " evens the trade." The balance of trade is the residue of indebtedness on one side or on the other, after particular balances are offset or cancelled. Banks perform this office* for individual traders, cities, and sections; clearing houses perform it for banks; the body of foreign bankers perform it for the foreign commerce of the country considered as a whole.

This explanation must render it clear that with all the wonderful expansion of industry and complication of trade which distinguish our times, the rudimentary forms still survive, the products of industry are still interchanged by processes which, when these products are reduced to their common denominator, value, are seen to be but barter amplified and grown intricate, as all the interlacing ramifications of the oak are developed from the bourgeoning of the sapling. This being the case, it follows that the principles of barter, of simple trade, must apply to all commercial and financial operations; that the ciphers which in notation distinguish 1,000,000 from 1, merely change the degree of whatever force the integer possesses— 1,000,000 dollars is simply one dollar raised to the millionth power, as a million bushels of wheat means one bushel repeated a million times. This is of importance because men speculating on financial matters are generally lifted above the solid ground of reason and fact by the efforts they make to climb what seem mountains in the clouds, when

* Of keeping accounts and settling balances.

they are really only the magnified and distorted simulacra of palpable and every-day experiences. The commerce of the country, though expressed in hundreds of millions of dollars, is made up wholly of transactions conducted by individuals; all of these are reducible, as we have seen, to a common denominator, value; hence in the aggregate they are subject to the laws and influences that apply to each separate transaction, and to none others. The practical conclusions that follow this view are of immense importance to all who desire to understand financial matters, for they supply the key to all the seeming mysteries of trade, both foreign and domestic, and to all the problems in banking and in national finance.

Value is the product of the opposite forces of demand and supply. Money is the conventional standard for measuring value. Commerce in exchanging commodities also effects an exchange of values, and finance adjusts and settles the balances arising in these exchanges.

CHAPTER XIX.

THE STANDARD OF VALUE

Ephron the Hittite, dwelling among the children of Heth, owned a field which Abraham, who had come to Hebron to bury Sarah, his wife, desired to buy for a sepulchre. Ephron pressed it upon him as a gift; Abraham insisted upon paying "the full money it is worth." Whereupon Ephron said, "The land is worth 400 shekels of silver." We do not know upon what ground Ephron spoke so decidedly as to the money value of his field; and we may well believe that Abraham's affliction put bargaining out of the question on both sides; but it is important to have this unique bit of evidence as to the definiteness and precision of the price of land so long ago. Whether the value of land in Hebron determined the value of silver there, whether the value of silver throughout Asia Minor was at that time so well established as to make it a familiar standard of value for all other things, or whether, lastly, there was some standard of value besides these, by which both land and silver were gauged, are questions which history does not solve, and upon which the Scripture narrative throws no light.

It is not surprising that this point is in doubt, for still, after 3,700 years of buying and selling, hiring, borrowing, trafficking, in every quarter of the globe, even now, when trade covers immense areas and is conducted under much stress of competition, we are ourselves at issue both as to what is and as to what should be the ultimate standard of value. We feel as much confidence as Ephron expressed as to the money our property is worth; we pay liberally to have quotations flashed from a thousand markets, that we may follow prices into minute fractions, and be sure what particular hundredth of a cent stood between buyers and sellers of wheat, cotton, or securities at the end of a day's bargaining. The funded debt of the civilized world, amounting probably to * $40,000,000,000, is predicated upon "value received" and agreed to be paid in like value; yet statesmen, financiers, and economists have been for a hundred years debating what is the standard of value, and are to-day undecided whether the labor that produces values is also the basis of their measurement, or whether values and labor, too, are measured by gold and silver.† In recent years another question has arisen, viz.,

---

* W. L. Fawcett: "Gold and Debt," p. 122. S. S. Griggs & Co., Chicago. 1887.

† The discussion as to labor and value finds its parallel in Mr. Froude's story of the owl which meditated incessantly upon the problem whether there was first an owl and then an egg, or first an egg and then an owl. The wise bird shuddered with dismay at the suggestion that the problem might some day be solved. "What, then, should we have to meditate upon?" he cries.

whether gold alone should or should not be made by law the sole standard of value.

Some readers may wonder whether it is really of any practical importance to have a standard of value at all, since the world seems to have got on without it for nearly forty centuries, but it is not said that the world has been without standards of value, only that we to-day are not agreed as to what is the standard now. There must always be a standard of value of some sort in the mind of every man who estimates the worth of a thing; consciously, or unconsciously, he must arrive at his estimate by a process of comparison with other values, and as trade involves appraisement of values by both seller and buyer, all traders are accustomed to effect such appraisements by using a mental value-scale. These mental value-scales are constructed by observation and experience as to current prices; hence they are marked off in the money denominations most familiar to each person. The degrees of our scales are dollars, dimes, and cents, and multiples or fractions of these; inhabitants of Great Britain and Ireland have their mental value-scales marked in pounds, shillings, and pence; the French use francs and centimes; the Germans, marks, etc. The money legalized by these countries is the standard of value recognized in the value-scales of its inhabitants, and if there were no communication, no commerce among and between the nations using these different value-scales, there would be no need of any standard of value common to all, for such a standard is required only to serve as a medium for comparing these different value-scales and constructing tables of their correspondences; such comparison being essential in order that commerce may effect industrial exchanges among these nations.

The existence of trade creates the need of a standard of value, and since trade at the present day is world-wide, there is now a necessity, not existing even a hundred years ago, for a world-wide standard of value. The primary idea of a standard involves its successive application to and comparison with the things to be measured, *i.e.*, those of which the weight, volume, or dimensions are to be determined, while its secondary force, that which distinguishes the standard from other implements of measurement, implies its employment exclusively to determine and to vouch the accuracy of such implements which, when proved accurate, represent the standard and may be used in place of it. These two meanings of the word arise out of and therefore follow, necessarily, the ordinary conduct of men. Millions of us buy and sell things by yards and pounds, bushels and gallons, and are content with the implements kept in the shop or those sold to us for use at home. We assume that they are correct, and make them the standards for all our measurements;—without recalling, even if we know, that the laws require implements of measurement to conform to certain standards carefully and accurately constructed, which are kept under lock and key at the National Museum at Washington.

So it is with our value-scales; we use dollars, etc., as measures of value, without reflecting that their usefulness for this purpose depends wholly upon their correspondence with the standard of value fixed by law, just as the usefulness of foot rules, quart measures, and pound weights depend upon their conformity with the legal standard of dimension and weight.

We have seen how in each country the monetary unit serves as a standard by which local money is maintained at uniform value, so that any of it may serve as a measure of value in the daily traffic of the people; and it has just been shown that the same principle requires that all nations that trade together must have a standard of value common to all. Under primitive social and industrial conditions the money in use is the sole standard of value. The idea of representative value, the use of instruments of credit as vehicles of value, belong to modern times and to advanced social and industrial development. Hence in ancient times and even now in countries only partially developed we find that the intrinsic value of the coined metal in circulation is the only standard of value, while in every highly developed country there are many forms of money in circulation having no intrinsic value and owing the stability of their money-force, the uniformity of their purchasing power, wholly to the relations they bear to a standard of value apart from themselves. Every standard of value is useful in proportion to the extent of the community which has adopted and recognized it. It is possible to adopt standards of value which answer, as well as one of the precious metals would, the purposes of a limited community.

The colonial history of the United States affords several instances of other substances besides metals serving for a number of years as money in the isolated communities of those times; but as areas of inter-communication became extended, and as the facilities of travel and transportation became improved, the conditions which alone underlie such use of an exceptional substance are found to be too unequally distributed to sustain their general adoption as a standard of value. It has been found, therefore, in all communities covering a considerable area and developing a high degree of industrial and commercial activity, that no standard of value remains permanently in use except it be one of the precious metals.

It has been established in Chapter XVI. of this treatise, that whatever settles balances at any focus of exchanges is alone competent to serve all the purposes of money throughout the area traversed by the transactions settled at that focus; hence, so far as the purely commercial aspect of the question is concerned, it would appear that all countries able to do so should make their monetary unit of gold, because gold alone settles balances in London, which, being at the focus of the world's exchanges, is the world's clearing-house. It is idle for us in the United States or for any other nation or set of nations to rebel against this requirement of commerce, because resistance is futile.

No particular nation or people can separate itself from others in respect to the medium for settling international balances, except under the penalty of commercial inferiority, if not isolation; for the condition of commercial fellowship among civilized nations is that each shall conform to the general practice of all. This principle asserts itself whenever communities, nations, races or still greater aggregations of men are animated by a common purpose or seek an end desired by all. The world fixes its own standards of government, statesmanship, jurisprudence, art, morality, military strategy, oratory, manners and customs. These have varied from age to age, and while many nations, cities, and individuals have doubtless participated in the choice and changes of type, yet in each age and on each line of social development some one people, some one city, even occasionally some individual, has been invested with the prestige of being the organ of the age for formulating and practically establishing the results of a prevailing tendency, and for supplying and preserving the type which best embodied those results.

In the course of time Nineveh, Babylon, Thebes,

Athens, Rome, Constantinople, Paris, London, have given law and have set fashions for the contemporaneous world, and this is solely because social forces always centre somewhere, and among the chief cities of each epoch that one becomes the world's centre which happens to stand nearest to the objective point of whatever social tendency is paramount among all such tendencies most widely prevailing at the time. War, religion, literature, art, manners, commerce, and finance, have had by turns, eras of supremacy among the objects of general human interest; each has made some great city the seat of its empire, and each has been advanced toward perfection by thus attracting to itself the concentrated efforts of mankind, and supplying a theatre for observation, comparison, and rivalry. In our age, finance rules the world, and London is its throne; finance holds supreme sway over values; hence its empire includes every man, woman, and child on the face of the earth who is engaged in industry or who is remotely dependent upon those so engaged, because industry must be ever producing values, and it is ever dependent upon finance for effecting the exchanges by which alone its products are distributed and its productive forces nourished. Lombard Street is the focus of those exchanges, and whatever measures values in Lombard Street must necessarily determine and control values wherever industry plies the plough, the pick, the hammer, the shuttle, or the yardstick.

Whether we consent or not, therefore, whether we approve or not, as long as the world has Lombard Street for its clearing-house, just so long must we conform to the standard of value there. It would seem to be as difficult to change the financial centre of the world as to change the location of the magnetic pole, and even a change of centre would not change the standard, if, as seems to be the case, that standard is the product of natural forces of world-wide effectiveness. The magnetic pole might be changed, but magnetism would remain unchanged.

The fact that London is to-day measuring values in gold, although values were once measured there in silver, suggests an inquiry as to whether formerly silver and now gold are ultimate standards, or whether these are merely implements of value-measurement based upon and conformed to some higher, broader, and more permanent standard, as the French standards or units of physical measurement are based upon geometrical data.

This opens up the question as to what is the true scientific standard of value. Since value is not a physical quality of objects, like extension and weight, but is a relation between certain things to which men attribute value, and the human beings whose needs and desires lead them to attribute value to those particular things, a scientifically adequate standard of values must be something that can be always and everywhere used with uniform precision for measuring and comparing different degrees of that relation. In seeking for such a standard, let us begin by inquiring what is the actual notion that underlies and sustains men's ideas of proportional values. In civilized countries money serves this purpose, and beyond the pale of civilization degrees of value are determined by differences in the risk of life or limb, or in the expenditure of vital energy which men are willing to incur in order to keep or to acquire that which they value.

We have, therefore, as natural standards of value, three classes of objects: human life, human labor and money, which last, to avoid an apparent *petitio principii*, may be merged into its generic, property. One of these classes must include some object fitted to be the standard of value, and no object will serve that purpose unless it fulfils the œcumenical conditions, *Semper, ubique, ab omnibus;* that is, it must "always, everywhere, and by all men" have been regarded as of prime value. Evidently, if such values exist, it is among them that we will find the standard we want. Human life naturally suggests itself as the highest of all natural values. Satan is reported in the book of Job as saying, "All that a man hath will he give for his life." And the saying suits its author, who is ever leading men astray by half-truths. If the saying is true as to some men, it is not true as to all, because there have always been and are still great numbers of men in every community ready to lay down their lives in defence of their property,* while many a miser, when ill, denies himself nourishment and medical relief, so that he dies, when he might prolong life by parting with a minute fraction of his treasures. If we consider the relative estimation in which men hold wealth and the lives of human beings remote from them, we shall find that human life in general is far less esteemed than wealth. Men and even women have been known to sacrifice the happiness or health, and even to imperil the lives, of their parents and their children, in order to preserve their wealth, and sometimes merely to increase it.

It appears, therefore, that while among men generally the greater number, perhaps, are so constituted that each holds his own life dearer than his property, yet even among these each esteems his own property as dearer to him than the life of another man, or even than the lives of numbers of other men; hence we must concede that human life, on the whole, is valued below property on the whole. Even if this were not so, human life could not serve as a standard of value, because there is no way of measuring values by lives, since we cannot barter lives experimentally, and since also there is no identity or equality of value between any two lives. Each man values his own higher than any number of lives in which he feels no interest, and he values the lives of others accord-

---

* If this were not so, burglars would thrive better, who habitually risk their lives, not to defend their own property, but to appropriate that of others.

ing to his interest in them severally; whereas a standard of value must be similarly esteemed by all men.

Quite a system of political economy has been constructed upon the dictum that human labor is the ultimate standard by which all values are determined. This is an attractive notion, and is convenient for demagogues; but it is not true, and it would be unfortunate if it were true, because there is no possible way of either defining the value of human labor in the abstract, or of applying human labor in the concrete, as a standard for measuring other values—say, for example, that of wheat. If one inquires how much human labor it takes to produce a bushel of wheat, any practical farmer will reply that it depends upon geographical location, soil, climate, drainage, the seed used, the time of planting, the machinery employed in preparing the land and in sowing, reaping, and threshing the grain, the fertilizers applied, the character of the season, and the quality of the labor. Here are a dozen distinct, essentially different elements, all of them variable through many degrees, which must be combined with human labor in order to produce wheat at all; and supposing the labor to be constant, the variations in the quantity of product possibly resulting from variations in these elements are immeasurable. But human labor itself is by no means a constant force, for it is affected by precisely those qualities, physical, intellectual, and moral, which distinguish individuals from each other. Hardly any two men are alike in build, activity, muscular development, nerve, endurance, intelligence, ingenuity, skill, experience, energy, and persistence — all qualities more or less affecting the amount and quality of work that a man can do in a given time; and since the value of labor depends upon the amount and quality of the work accomplished, and upon the time it takes to do it, the labor of different men must vary in value according to the degree in which they severally possess these different qualities, and according to the incentive to, and the need of, or the opportunity for, exercise of them in the work to be done. The same man cannot count upon doing as much or doing it as well one day with another.

Even the lowest and rudest forms of labor fail to supply a basis for values, because both the object to which, and the manner in which, any amount of labor is applied exercise an influence upon the resulting product, and it is not until labor results in some product that the labor can be gauged as to value. It is very different as to horse-power, a mere conventional term for a unit of force, which is measured quite otherwise than by the actual exertion of a horse. Human labor in the abstract cannot be similarly conventionalized, averaged, as it were, into a certain modicum available as a unit of value. If anyone thinks otherwise, let him study Sir Thomas Brassey's observations as to the relative value of laborers classed as to race, habits, and habitation, and also according to the character of the work to be done.

But if it were possible to obtain a modicum of human labor that could pass as a conventional unit of value, how could such a unit be applied to the measurement of values generally? The conventional unit of force called one-horse power will invariably, at ordinary altitudes, anywhere in the world, lift the same weight so many feet in a second of time; but there is no kind or amount of human labor that will produce, in the same time and under like conditions, at Calcutta what the same kind and amount produces in New York, whether measured in wages or in any other way. How, then, could any given modicum of labor be used in either of these places to measure the value there of the products of the same modicum of labor performed at the other place?

Again, if human labor were the standard by which all values adjusted themselves or are adjusted, then, certainly, the same man ought to command everywhere identical value for his labor, or, at least, his labor ought to be approximately equal in value wherever and however employed; whereas we know as a fact that this is not so, but that the direct contrary is true, viz., that almost every man can earn more and do better for himself in one place, or in one employment, than in any other. This truth is the foundation of Adam Smith's practical exposition of what he termed the division of labor; it is the keystone to the philosophical doctrine of free trade, and it utterly excludes from possibility of verity the theory that human labor is the ultimate standard of value.*

The fact is that in some ages of the world human labor had no value whatever, and this is the case even now in some regions, while in those ages and regions other values existed and exist. † Labor came to have distinct value only after mankind had progressed out of the patriarchal conditions, for before that the man's labor was merged in his personality, and the benefit derived from it inured to the possessor of his person. If he were the head of a house, his labor was his own, so were also its fruits; if he were a minor, a dependent, or a slave, his labor and its fruits, as well as his person, belonged to the head of the house.

At that very time, however, men dealt in values; money was known and used; its functions were the same in the essential elements as they are to-day. Ephron's field was worth 400 shekels of silver. What human labor served as a common standard of value, recognized by Abraham and by the children of Heth as well? Consider the nomadic, the predatory, the pastoral tribes scattered over the world; they have no conception of the value of human labor, no means of estimating how much labor enters into the values obtained by them in fight, in trade, or by the fecundity of their flocks

---

* It is surprising that Adam Smith failed to see this incongruity.

† See "In Darkest Africa," H. M. Stanley.

and herds; yet they have definite ideas of value, both positive and relative. The wretched remnants of the aboriginal races of America hold labor in contempt, though encompassed by a people who exult in it; yet they understand values. It is useless to multiply arguments; the hypothesis that human labor is or can be made a standard by which to measure the value of property, is untenable in reason, is inconsistent with industrial facts, and is contradicted by our commonest experiences.*

Since neither human life nor human labor can

---

* The unphilosophical assumption that labor is, or should be, the standard of value seems to have had its origin in the recognition of labor as the essential factor in the production of wealth. Up to the time of Adam Smith, economists had generally considered that all value came out of the earth, and while they recognized the usefulness of the various handicrafts, and were beginning to discern the importance of machinery in the production of wealth, they had not formed a logical bridge between the old dogmas and the newly recognized facts of political economy.

Smith discovered and established the doctrine of labor-value in utilizing the forces of nature; he revealed to his generation the immortal truth that the ploughman is more productive than the soil, the reaper of more importance than standing corn, that the fisherman and not the sea supplies the market with fish, and that it is the delver and not the mine that gives us coal and metals for use.

Naturally and pardonably, he magnified the offspring of his genius. Labor being the creator of value, why should it not also be its gauge and standard? He assumes this hastily, and evidently never saw the inconsistency between that assumption and his magnificent demonstration of the doctrine which he called " the division of labor."

Now, to deny that human labor is a practicable standard of value is not to belittle, but to exalt, the function of labor in the be used as a standard of value, we must look for that standard among the various forms of property, and especially among the substances to which mankind has everywhere and always attributed the highest value as objects both of possession and of pursuit. The standard we are seeking must be among these, because being held in nearly the same degree of estimation by all men, they are the most constant objects of that relation between human desire and external matter which is expressed by the term value; one of these, therefore, can alone fulfil the conditions essential to a standard of value.

Now, when we consult history, we find that there is not only one such substance, but there are many; they are comprised within two classes, precious stones and precious metals. It is characteristic of precious stones that each is a gem, complete in

production of wealth. Surely that which creates is greater than that which measures. And where shall we find, either in the economy of nature or in the practice of mankind, any precedent for assuming that the force that produces can be made to measure the product? There is no proportion between the oak and the acorn from which it sprang; the mariner does not compute the progress of his ship by the velocity of the wind that fills its sails; nor does the machinist use the expansive force of steam as the unit for measuring the stroke of the trip-hammer.

The military force that held Thermopylæ would have been swept away by a Gatling gun. Should we take that as a standard for measuring the effect of the defence upon the whole course of European history? or is it conceivable that there is any possible basis for comparative commensuration, by military, moral, or ethnic force, between the effects of our Revolutionary War and those of the tremendous Franco-Teutonic struggle?

itself—individual, single, inviolate. Each gem has to be valued singly, according to its individual properties and defects; and different kinds of gems, even individual specimens of the same kind, are variously estimated by men of various tastes; hence, while as a class they may be the most precious of substances, yet, on account of their peculiarities, no one of the precious stones is fit to be used as a standard of value.

Again, since values differ among themselves by degrees, since they rise and fall by gradation, a standard of value must be capable of systematic and accurate subdivision, without loss of value; but precious stones cannot be fused together so as to equalize their properties, nor can they be subdivided without destruction both of their substance and of their value. Such adaptability to subdivision must apply not only to the mass, but also to those qualities of the substance in which its value inheres, so that, of any two equal quantities of the substance selected as a standard of value, either will be worth as much as the other, and any fraction of one of these quantities will be equal in value to a like fraction of the other. This property of continuous divisibility, without loss of characteristics or value, is entirely absent from precious stones, but it is the distinguishing quality of all metals which are capable of being brought into a state of uniform purity.

We have already seen that many different substances have been used as money, and that all have been forsaken for metals, as communities advanced in industrial development. Even under present conditions, it is conceivable that the world might get on with a standard of value based on one of the grosser metals, such as iron, tin, or copper, because those metals possess value and also the property of accurate subdivision; but since the number of metals affords a choice among them, that choice has fallen finally upon silver and gold. It is obvious that, in fixing upon silver and gold to be standards of value, modern nations have simply followed a natural law, because these metals have always been, and are everywhere, regarded by all men with the highest degree of estimation, *i.e.*, they have been more constantly and more universally than all other metals, objects of that relation which is designated by the term value, and hence are the best fitted to be exponents of value.

At the present day, even, there is a divergence. Among some nations silver is the accepted standard of value; elsewhere gold is the standard; while the nations of the Latin Union maintained for many years a dual standard (or, as the advocates of that system call it, a double standard), composed of gold and silver, in the proportion, as to value, of one unit of gold to 15½ units of silver. At present the tendency seems to be toward the general adoption of gold as the sole standard among the most advanced nations, and many persons think this tendency should be arrested—some urging that the use of silver and gold jointly should be secured by an international agreement; and others advocating even the free coinage of silver in this country alone, at the present rate of 412½ grains, 900 fine, to the dollar. It is a question of momentous consequence, because if the bi-metallists are right, there is a fatal malady in the very heart of the whole social and industrial structure of the civilized world; while if they are wrong, their efforts may undermine and wreck that structure to no purpose.

The discussion of bi-metallism, however, cannot be undertaken here. The purpose of this treatise confines it to the exposition of those principles which should be known to, and respected by, those who control our money and monetary affairs; because they are principles which take their rise in the nature of things, and give vitality to the natural laws which must eventually determine our prosperity, in spite of legislative or administrative direction or obstruction.

Without reference, therefore, to the questions raised by the bi-metallists, let us proceed to inquire how it has come about that the world is now gravitating toward the single gold standard. We have already seen that universal industry produces universal commerce; universal commerce requires a world's clearing-house; London is the clearing-house; in London gold is the money of ultimate settlement, and all the advanced countries of the world seem to be under compulsion to adopt the same usage. Now, why does London insist on gold?

CHAPTER XX.

THE GOLD STANDARD

The gold standard has not been established by measures designed to bring about that result, but it has come into use under the influence of commercial forces, which in their origin, nature, and effect were altogether independent of any reasoning or theorizing as to the material of money or the measurement of values. These commercial forces were engendered by the momentous industrial changes that have occurred during the nineteenth century, and they received their energy and were determined in the direction of their influence by the extension of civilization, the spread of industry, the diversification of employments, the multiplication of products, the expansion of consumption, the improvements in transportation, and the marvellous increase in the rapidity of communication, and in the volume of trade and traffic, which have taken place during the last fifty years.

The adoption of gold as the sole standard of value, wherever these changes have occurred, is just as natural, as inevitable, and as final an outcome of such changes as are the substitution of steam-power for horses in land transportation and for sails in navigation; the substitution of gas and electricity for whale-oil and candles in illumination; the substitution of iron and steel for wood in ship-building; and the change from old and unsatisfactory devices to the present systems of post-office, police, and fire department organization and equipment. None of these substitutions occurred suddenly. They were at first proposed by theorists, and were long contended for in argument; but in all cases they worked their own way slowly, by experiment at obscure initial points, widely apart, and are established now only because they are the best things of their several kinds that the world has had any knowledge of, and they are destined, no doubt, in their turn to be supplanted by other things now unknown and undreamed of.

Each one of these new devices encountered opposition, and even denunciation; each affected injuriously the industries and fortunes of individuals and communities; each was delayed and obstructed by ignorance and prejudice; each was more costly than that which it supplanted; but all are now recognized as so many achievements in the progress of mankind from the inferior and primitive toward the modern and superior conditions of individual well-being and social elevation. The communities that earliest adopted these improvements have longest enjoyed their benefits, and have thereby become recognized as among the advanced communities of the world. Those that have not yet adopted them are laggards in civilization.

To understand how the adoption of the single

gold standard is related to all these other substitutions of the new and better for the old and worse, will be found easy enough if one bears in mind the principles which have been set out and illustrated in the preceding chapters of this treatise—principles drawn from what Montesquieu calls "the nature of things." Let us review these briefly. 1. The principle that progress in respect to the material of money has always been, and must always be, from less valuable to more valuable substances. (Chap. IV.) 2. The principle that confidence is a *sine qua non* of the monetary efficiency of any circulating medium. (Chap. VI.) 3. The principle that definiteness and stability of value are indispensable qualities of money. (Chap. VIII.) 4. The principle that only money good everywhere, within a given area of industry or trade, is available in the settlements of balances at the point upon which the exchanges of that area are centred. (Chap. XVI.) 5. The principle that there can be but one standard of value in any such area. (Chap. XIX.)

The first principle has for its logical sequence the practical maxim, that the material of highest intrinsic value used as money in any community, becomes necessarily the standard of value there. *

---

* It is interesting to observe that this result of the principle in question is the exact complement of Gresham's Law. According to this law, the inferior elements of a mixed currency obtain the most rapid circulation, while according to the natural law here set forth, only the higher elements of a currency become available for settling balances among banks and bankers.

There can be no doubt that where these two opposing laws are

Taking the civilized and commercial nations of the world which settle their trade balances in London as one community, and recognizing, as we must, that an ounce of gold is of higher intrinsic value than an ounce of silver, copper, or nickel (the only other money metals now in use), it is evident that, according to the maxim just stated, gold of necessity must be the standard of value in London.

The second principle is that nothing can pass as money unless there is confidence in the future continuity of its efficiency as a medium of purchase and payment. This principle precludes the use as international money of any metal but gold, because each of the other money metals has forfeited that confidence by having become, somewhere and at some time, inefficient as a medium for the settlement of international balances, while gold has steadfastly maintained its efficiency in that regard everywhere and at all times.

The third principle requires gold because that metal alone has remained definite and stable in purchasing power.*

---

allowed free play they tend to neutralize each other, and to preserve all the elements of a mixed currency at a uniform value ; for, although each law is constantly operative to sift out in a discriminating way the better from the worse elements, yet through the return flow of exchanges the elements of the two currents become again mingled together in the general circulation.

* It used to be contended by some that gold has advanced in purchasing power, and that silver alone has been stab'e in that respect ; but since the great decline in the value of silver in the last few years we hear no more of that contention.

The fourth and fifth principles obviously make gold the only logical money in London, because (1) it is the most valuable of the money metals; (2) it alone possesses the confidence of all nations in respect to the permanency of its value; and (3) according to commonly accepted methods of computation, gold has been more definite and stable in value than any other substance used as money anywhere in the world. While it is evident that "the nature of things" is responsible for the use of gold as the sole medium of settlement in London, it may be interesting to follow the process by which the transition from silver to gold has been effected.

The changes mentioned above as having been wrought during the present century, have reduced all values except the value of human endeavor, but this last has never before been so well compensated as it is now. Whether we consider wages or commercial profits, or professional emoluments, or the riches acquired by invention, speculation, or what is euphemistically termed "handling properties," we will find that they have been upon a steadily advancing scale of value, and that the time and talents and efforts of men were never so highly paid for as they are now; and since, simultaneously, all other things have been cheapened, the earnings of men bring them in vastly more in all articles of need, of comfort, and of luxury than could have been acquired by the same effort at any previous time.

Concurrently with the enhancement in value of

individual exertion, there has been an immeasurable increase in the number of men, women, and children who participate in these increased profits, and for whose continuous employment and maintenance there must be innumerable currents of trade kept running in every direction. Now, it has been shown in Chap. I. that for every such current of trade there is a counter-current of exchange setting toward some money centre, and from every money centre similar but larger currents flow toward London (directly or through intermediate points of settlement); so that London is at the present day the centre of centres for the settlement of balances—the clearing-house of the commerce of the world.

London has not always occupied this position, nor did that city attain it suddenly. The currents of trade, on the one hand, and of exchanges that now centre there, on the other, have not sprung into existence all at once; they have gradually been developed out of a number of little, sluggish movements conducted by means of the inferior appliances of our great-grandfathers—the pack-horse first, then the wagon, the sailing-ship, the caravan, the post-rider, the canal-boat, etc., in transportation, and all sorts of money and substitutes for money in settlements and exchanges. With the progress of the century and the improvements in appliances, these movements broadened and deepened and produced others of like character; the channels through which they were conducted became more defined, more direct and safer, and the volume of each movement became more constant; hence gradually the clearings at money centres became greater in volume, and settlements between cities and sections required the use of larger and larger amounts of money, and exacted money of the best quality obtainable within the limits of the district.

At first the trade and exchanges of each district constituted a separate system, and some town became the district centre; then there arose dealings between people in some districts and those in others, and these were settled at some one point—never at more than one—which might or might not have been a district centre; and so, as these movements became extended and ramified and interlaced, new centres replaced old ones; but always there were fewer and fewer centres, and always each new centre was a bigger and richer place than that it supplanted; and always, also, the settlements at the new points necessitated the use of more money, and of the best money obtainable anywhere within the enlarged area.

Now, as long as there were a multitude of little trade districts scattered over Europe and North America, there might have been almost as many distinct monetary systems, because each district centre was to a great extent independent of others; but as the districts grew into sections and the sections became multiplied, and as, afterward, sectional trade limits faded, and in each country one national centre took the place of many sectional and district centres, it became necessary to unify, both in form and in value, the money in use within each of these constantly expanding trade peripheries; and at each step in monetary reform the standard selected for the enlarged area was in fact, and had to be, in economical logic, that form of money which compressed the highest value into the least mass. Among other reasons for this, one of the most practicable and intelligible is economy in transportation of the medium of settlement. As long as it is cheaper to transport 1,000 ounces of gold than 16,000 ounces of silver, and as long as these two masses of metal are of equal value, it is obvious that persons having to remit specie will send gold rather than silver; and as the distance to the point of settlement increases, the advantages of gold shipments over silver must increase proportionately.

In early days obstructions to transportation were so great that values in any one place maintained a degree of stability impossible under present conditions. Areas of reciprocal trade were circumscribed and the barriers of nature were so effective that commerce could break through them at only a few points and by methods both tedious and costly. Robbers infested the overland routes, pirates roamed the seas; hence overland transportation was dependent upon caravans under military escort, and marine commerce was hazardous beyond modern comprehension.

The result of this general condition was that the industrial world was made up of numerous distinct communities, with but little local trade in any, and very meagre intercourse with each other. Under such conditions the stock of money in each of these communities was of small value and consisted of numerous pieces of minute denomination. Silver was the only precious metal cheap enough to serve as a multiple of these minute monetary values, and the obstacles to transportation kept each community's stock of silver nearly constant in quantity, and consequently nearly stable in value. If there had been any use for gold as money in such communities the stock would have been more variable, because value is more portable in gold than in silver, and consequently its value as a basis would have been less stable.

The present condition is the opposite of that then existing, for now industry is coextensive with civilization, and commerce is almost universal, so that there is hardly anywhere a community without trade, or beyond the influence of the world's commerce. This condition of industry and trade necessitates incessant settlement of balances between trade centres, and these balances are very large in amount—so that gold now derives its equability of value from its superior portability because transportation facilities are so universal and so cheap that the slightest elevation of value at one point sets in motion currents of supply from many other points, and the effect is the preservation of the world's stock of gold at very nearly the same value everywhere.

Silver, as a standard of value within circumscribed and barrier-bound limits, bears to gold as the general standard, now that the barriers are removed, a relation like that which lakes bear to the ocean as sources of moisture supply and objective points of drainage. For its own district each lake suffices as a reservoir for receiving the excessive rainfall and yielding it back to the clouds, but for equalizing and distributing the world's supply of moisture, oceans alone suffice.

The natural laws that control the currents of the air, and the formation and condensation of clouds, are not more constant than are the natural laws that control the currents of commerce, and the distribution of capital.* It is natural law alone that has gradually made gold the prime standard of value. Thus it came about that Great Britain was the first nation to adopt the single gold standard (1816), while for a long time afterward other nations did very well without it. The principal countries of Continental Europe were commercially isolated by the protective system, and their bi-metallic currencies supplied not only the needs of domestic circulation, but gold for trade with gold countries, and silver for trade with the South and East.

* The efforts now being made to preserve the monetary use of silver in international trade are on a level with the pranks of Dyrenforth, and are destined to a like failure.

Before the advent of ocean steamers the United States were geographically isolated; hence here, too, there was for a time a bi-metallic circulation: for we used gold to settle Canadian and European balances and silver to settle balances arising in the trade with Central and South America and the West Indies. The debasing of the gold standard in 1834 drove our silver coins abroad, and from that time we were practically on a gold basis until 1860; but to-day commerce has brought all nations into one monetary community, and forces upon all, in "the nature of things," the use of one and the same standard of value. It is the operation of natural law alone that brought gold coins into use in Italy when the little States of the Peninsula became united into a kingdom, that demonetized silver in Central Europe when Prussia expanded into the Empire of Germany, and that closed the mints of the Latin Union to the coinage of silver when the Franco-Prussian war left France a Republic, with her enormous industrial forces stimulated to activity by the depletion wrought by the contest, and set free from the trammels and burdens of Imperial centralism and extravagance.

Silver now suffices as a standard of value in Mexico, Central and South America, and Asia, because these countries are still in a comparatively primitive state of industrial development; but Japan has adopted the single gold standard, and in India there are already signs that industry, expanded and better organized, is outgrowing the silver stage—and if her commerce were not so largely confined to Great Britain, India would now find it necessary to adopt the gold standard also.

At the beginning of the nineteenth century Great Britain was by far the foremost commercial nation of the world, and there industry was more active and diversified, labor was better compensated and consumption more extended than anywhere else; hence it is in accordance with the principles stated above that Great Britain should have early adopted the single gold standard. It seems now as if the statesmen who were instrumental in bringing about the new Coinage Law (of Great Britain), in 1816, had a very imperfect understanding of the influences constraining them to that course; but they felt the need of doing something, and if Lord Liverpool had not hit upon the right expedient, some subsequent premier would certainly have done so, under the guidance of clearer views as to the effect of the establishment of the single gold standard upon the foreign commerce of Great Britain, and upon the future position of London toward the world's commerce.

Next to Great Britain the United States became, early in the century, the country of greatest and most diversified industrial and commercial activity, and consequently, in 1834, this country adopted in fact, though Congress did not establish by law, the single gold standard. As apparently in England, so certainly here, the change was effected by men having quite other ends in view. To encourage and reward the gold miners of the United States, it was said, the pure gold in the dollar was reduced from 24.75 to 23.22 grains. This change, as was intended, gave the miners more dollars to the ounce than they were getting before; but as the silver dollars were not changed in weight, the relative value of the two metals in our currency was reversed, and silver dollars disappeared from circulation. This result evidently was neither foreseen nor desired, but it was universally accepted without remonstrance, because no doubt no one was thereby hurt or inconvenienced.

Up to 1834, gold coins could not circulate in the United States, and the country was practically on the silver basis. After 1834, silver dollars could no longer circulate, and the country had only the gold standard up to the suspension of specie payment at the outbreak of the Civil War—a period of nearly twenty-eight years—during which the United States gained more in industrial development, commercial extension, population, and a generally diffused prosperity of the people, than in all their previous existence.

In 1871, and while specie payments in the United States were still suspended, Germany attempted to substitute gold coins for silver coins in the monetary circulation of the Empire, and her sales of silver produced a disturbance in the European markets which caused France at first to restrict her coinage of silver, and finally to discontinue it altogether. This restriction began in France in 1873, and in the same year the United States so revised their coinage laws as to close their mints to the free coinage of silver. Not to have done so would have had the effect, when resumption took place, of substituting the silver standard for the gold (not in law, but in fact, inverting the action taken in 1834). No doubt resumption would have been rendered much easier under the silver than it could be under the gold standard, and no doubt also Germany would have been very glad to have sent her thalers to our mints, and to have taken in their place the gold which our Government subsequently accumulated in this country by the sale of bonds; and further, it may be conceded to be probable that in that case no one in Europe would now be discussing the silver question, because the nations of the Latin Union would have been able to keep their silver coinage within safe limits by adopting our ratio of 16 to 1, and then there would have been no silver question there, but where would we have been? What would it have profited us to have changed places with Germany—becoming silver mono-metallic in order that she might be gold mono-metallic? What good would it have done for us that the Latin Union could have safely drifted under the gold standard, in fact, while maintaining bi-metallism in law, as we did after 1834?

The same inevitable law that imposed the gold standard on Great Britain in 1816, that maintained it in this country from 1834 to 1862, that forced it upon Japan as soon as that singular kingdom sprung into commercial life, and that impelled Bismarck to try to establish it the moment Germany became an Empire, would have been at work among us driving us by the scourges of industrial depression and disorder toward our proper destiny as the controlling gold standard country of the world. We know what the country has gained under the gold standard since 1879. No one can compute what we might have lost if we had been during the same period on the monetary plane of India, Mexico, and China, with all industrial Europe raised to the higher level of the gold standard, and kept there by the weight of our silver circulation, bearing down the other end of the lever.

It would have been easier for us to have resumed specie payments in 1879, in silver, rather than in gold, just as climbing a low hill is easier than climbing a high mountain; but for a nation that is impelled both by ambition and by destiny to stand upon the highest elevation of human attainment in commerce and industry, it would be a monstrous blunder, a crime against our own posterity, for us now voluntarily to descend from the position we have attained with so much sacrifice and at so great cost. Gold mono-metallism is the unavoidable destiny of this country; the sooner we recognize this and fix it in our laws, the sooner will we reap the fruits; the longer we defer the recognition, the more we impede and postpone its establishment by law—the longer will our industries be hampered and all our business deranged by financial unrest and commercial apprehension. Should we unfortunately let go the single gold standard, there will be nothing to take hold of but silver mono-metallism, for bi-metallism for us is a snare and a delusion.

France stands next to the United States in the order of modern industrial progress; and had it not been for the unsettled social and political state of that country, terminating, as it did, in an unfortunate and disastrous war with Germany, France would probably have made more decided advance than she has done toward the single gold standard of value.

The monetary troubles of France began when the revolution of 1789 was being engendered by the follies and excesses of absolutism; their first phase culminated in the issue of assignats, in December of that year; and when order was reestablished it was found convenient to adopt what has been called the double standard of value a purely doctrinaire device, which became practicable only because of the geographical position of France, midway between the populations of eastern and southern Europe, and of Asia, which were all silver basis people, on the one side, and on the other, Great Britain, with the other gold-basis nations of northern Europe. From what precedes, it would appear that France is destined eventually to be driven to the gold standard—and all western Europe must follow. Russia, Turkey, and their dependencies cannot adopt it for many years to come. They, with Asia and Africa, South and Central America, must remain silver mono-metallic countries, because in none of these, except possibly India, is industry as yet sufficiently vigorous and sufficiently free to need or to use gold.

CONCLUSION

It is to be hoped that the reader who has followed the train of explanations and reasoning laid down in the preceding pages, will have acquired sufficient interest in the subject to feel a desire to test the writer's accuracy by observing more closely than he has before done, those movements of money, or of trade, that pass daily before his eyes. Such observation, it is believed, will establish the main propositions here stated; and if this be so, then it must follow that it is of supreme importance for these propositions to be generally understood and accepted by the great body of our citizens.

In the United States nearly everyone is in some way connected with or dependent upon industry. Variety of soil, climate, and occupations, create and sustain an immense internal trade. The bounty of nature, the energy and enterprise of our people, have built up a vast foreign commerce. We have a great capital invested in farm improvements, in live stock, in mining appliances, in banking institutions, in manufacturing establishments, in railroads, canals, and vessels, all dependent for profitable employment upon the activity of trade and commerce.

The revenues of the general government are mainly derived from taxes upon imports. The finances of states, counties, and cities rest upon a basis of values that cannot be maintained unless the currents of trade run freely. Probably no country in the world is so bound up in industry as this is; certainly in none are there so many individuals, in proportion to the whole population, engaged in working for themselves, and so many who habitually buy most of what they consume and sell most of what they produce. At the same time, never before have manufactures, trade, and transportation entered so largely into the employments of the world at large, nor has commerce ever been so broadly extended as it is now, or so sensitive at every point throughout its extension to the influence of local incidents, and even to the actions and opinions of individuals. The perceptions or the apprehensions of a few money magnates are reflected in the movements of capital, and the prices of securities at the chief financial centres; these centres in turn control the rates of interest, and affect the facility of loans all over Europe, and North America, and variations in these rates and facilities accelerate or retard the currents of trade, and excite or depress industrial activity throughout the whole world.

While commerce is thus daily and hourly affected by impulses proceeding from the great centres, it is much more affected by the reciprocal play of influences arising within its own proper sphere.

Universality of trade, celerity of communication, the organization of speculation, and the facility of transportation, have covered a large part of the earth's habitable surface with a network of mercantile operations, each connected with all the others as if by the interweaving of threads. Unnumbered commercial influences converge at every point where trade is going on, and at every such point fresh influences of greater or less intensity are generated or developed and radiate in all directions. The buyer and seller of wheat in Chicago, of cotton in Bombay, of wool at Cape Town, stand at the crossing of threads which are beaded with similar transactions extending from Odessa to San Francisco, from Canton to New Orleans, from Melbourne to Milwaukee; and every dealer in these articles receives, consciously or unconsciously, some impulse from every transaction, wherever it may occur.

The influence of organized speculation upon markets and trade, communicated through a wonderfully intricate and minute system of telegraphic reports, renders the vast network of commerce a living tissue, throbbing with thought and feeling along every line of electric communication. Currents of trade run through its veins and arteries at the speed of the locomotive and steamship, while the volume of each current varies incessantly with ever-changing impressions and opinions. The fluctuating desires, needs, and means of individual producers and consumers, constitute the capillaries of the system, and control the force and volume of these currents; activity and rapidity of production and consumption accelerate their flow, while opposite conditions retard it.

Money is the lubricant of this vast expanse of complicated machinery; it is money alone that can produce free movement at and between the initial and the ultimate points of every industrial effort, for it constitutes the wages of production, it defrays the cost of transportation, it pays the price of consumption. If at any of these points the supply of money is insufficient in quantity or defective in quality, friction ensues, and influences injurious to industry are instantaneously transmitted from that point along the unnumbered lines diverging from it. If the points so affected are numerous—and still more—if all the points in a great area are similarly affected, the trouble is aggravated in a multiplied ratio, and its effects extend further, and last longer.

Under normal conditions, credit supplements the use of money in transactions of considerable magnitude. At the great centres of trade and in the extended operations of intersectional, international, and intercontinental commerce, credit performs the same functions that money does in minor transactions, and at primary and ultimate points. If every cargo shipped to Europe had to be paid for in money brought thence for the purpose, the vast traffic of the ocean would stand still. If credit should so decline as to prevent the negotiation of domestic and foreign bills of exchange, the railroads, the manufactories, all the appliances, all the capital, and all the labor employed in the fabrication and transportation of commodities, would become as idle as a locomotive without fuel. But while credit supplements the use of money, the maintenance of credit absolutely depends upon a supply of money held in reserve, ready and sufficient to liquidate whatever balances result from its varied operations. Each individual must have money enough to keep his bank account good; every bank must have enough to settle its balances at the clearing-house; the Treasury must have enough to meet every engagement of Government; the country must have enough to settle any adverse balance arising in the foreign trade. The penalty for failure in each of these cases is discredit, and discredit causes commercial and financial disability.

The foreign trade of the country, aggregating annually in exports and imports of merchandise, $1,800,000,000 of value, is carried on almost wholly on credit. Whatever balances result from the operations which are represented by this vast sum must be met in money, and the money for that purpose must always be at hand and available, or else the whole fabric will feel the shock of that revulsion which proceeds from discredit.

From this glance at the money and credit system of the country, it is evident that every person has a direct and almost vital interest in its being as perfect as knowledge and experience can make it and in its being maintained always in thorough working order. In this view is it not the duty of those who understand the subject to say to the public: If you consult science in order to be sure that you have the best lubricant for your watches, your sewing-machines, and your steam-engines; if you employ architects to arrange, at considerable cost, the flues and pipes by which air, heat, and water are made to circulate most conveniently through your dwellings and public buildings, surely you cannot afford to be indifferent to the quality, the supply, or the regulation of the money which lubricates all the machinery of domestic, industrial, and national life, which sustains and facilitates the circulation of all the products of labor, all the objects of consumption and accumulation; for these and these alone freight your vessels and cars, fill your stores and warehouses, and contain within themselves both the seeds and the fruit of individual and national prosperity? In the present state of the world good money, honest money, alone can supply the means and secure the ends of civilized existence, and of personal and domestic happiness, and such money can be secured only by measures in harmony with those natural laws which God has ordained for the guidance of mankind.

THE END.

www.ingramcontent.com/pod-product-compliance
Lightning Source LLC
Chambersburg PA
CBHW031327230426
43670CB00006B/268